303 TRICKY CHECKMATES

ABOUT THE AUTHORS

FRED WILSON

Fred Wilson is among the finest chess teachers and authors. He has authored three books, *A Picture History of Chess, 101 Questions on How to Play Chess,* and *202 Surprising Mates* (with Bruce Alberston), and edited two others, *Classical Chess Matches:1907-1913,* and *Lesser-Known Chess Masterpieces: 1906-1915.* He is also the owner of Fred Wilson Chess Books in New York City.

BRUCE ALBERSTON

Bruce Alberston is a well-known chess trainer and teacher in the New York city area and has recently written and narrated the best-selling CD-ROM, *Quick Kills on the Chessboard,* and collaborated with Fred Wilson on *202 Surprising Mates.* Alberston did significant research and analysis for Bruce Pandolfini (who has written 17 books for Simon & Shuster).

303 TRICKY CHECKMATES

FRED WILSON & BRUCE ALBERSTON

CARDOZA PUBLISHING

ACKNOWLEDGMENTS
A special thanks to the beautiful and mysterious Riley Kellogg who checked, corrected, proofed, and solved. But mostly it was Riley who spun her magic and made the computer hum to her tune. Others who contributed positions, checked solutions, or made useful suggestions include: Adam Marcus, Tom Schrade, Jeff Ivins, Mike Senkiewicz, Emmit Jefferson, Michele Lance, Jeff Tannenbaum, Sari Glickstein, Steve Anderson, Ben Schanback, Jeremy Gross, Julian Katz-Samuels, Dan Satterwaite, Michael Puopolo, Alex Jarrell, Glen Hart, Andy Fox, Andy Ansell, Oshon Temple, Peter Winik, Nathan Resika, Alex Rasic, Ned Wall, and Peter J. Tamburro, Jr.

PRINTING HISTORY

| First Printing | January 1999 |
| Second Printing | February 2000 |

Library of Congress Catalogue Card No: 98-71037
ISBN: 158042-010-9

CARDOZA PUBLISHING
P.O. Box 1500 Cooper Station, New York, NY 10276
Phone (718)743-5229 • Fax (718)743-8284
email: cardozapub@aol.com
www.cardozapub.com

Write for your free catalogue of gaming and chess books, equipment, advanced strategies, and computer games.

TABLE OF CONTENTS

INTRODUCTION

*A thorough understanding of the typical mating continuations makes the most sacrificial combinations leading up to them not only not difficult, but almost a matter of course. – **Tarrasch***

*It is a mistake to think that combination is is solely a question of talent, and that it cannot be acquired. – **Reti***

"I can't believe I missed a mate in two!" How many, many times have you said this to yourself during your chessplaying career? Too often, I bet. Deep down you know that missed tactical threats or opportunities are the biggest hindrance to your improvement at chess.

Recently, one of us, Fred Wilson, reached the following position as White:

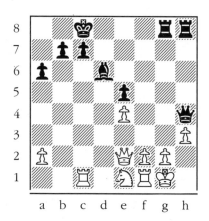

White, although a Pawn ahead, has a difficult position because of Black's heavy artillery on the g and h files, pointing at his King. Among Black's threats, were it his move, are 1... Qxh3 with a winning attack. White's g Pawn is pinned against his King by the Black Rook on g8.

White had a choice between 1. Qf3, which, although it defends against possible sacrifices on g2, does lose the h Pawn to 1... Qxh3! 2. Qxh3 Rxh3, and the seemingly safe, 1. Kh1, which is what he did.

What would you do now if you were Black?

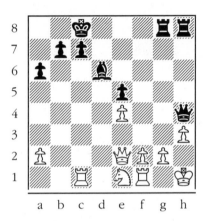

Answer: **1... Qxh3+! gxh3 2. Rxh3#.** That's right! An experienced player fell into a classic *corridor mate*, wherein the doomed King is mated by a major piece (Queen or Rook) on a rank or file, because there are no legal escape squares on the adjacent ranks or files, and no possible interpositions.

The possibility of this classic mating pattern, (like the notorious *back rank mate* except here mate occurs on the h file rather then the 1st or 8th rank,) should have been recognized by White, even if it was brought about by a Queen sacrifice!

So, what's the answer? How can we learn to stop overlooking mating combinations available to us, and threatened against us? There is only one way: to study different types of checkmating combinations over and over again until we are thoroughly familiar with the tactics and typical groups of pieces involved in successfully implementing them.

While in the past, it was believed that the ability to create attractive checkmating combinations must be a born gift, nowadays modern teaching experience has established that consistent training through solving standard checkmating positions, no matter how difficult, will improve any player's "feel" for discovering correct, and even brilliant, checkmating attacks.

What we have done in *303 Tricky Checkmates* is to assemble a collection of *forced* checkmates in 2, 3 and 4 moves, which we believe you will find both instructive and entertaining. We have purposely used very large, clear diagrams so you will not be discouraged from really trying to visualize possible variations.

We have also intentionally included 100 positions (mates 101-150 and 251-300), in which Black is to play and force checkmate in two or three moves. We believe it is essential that you become comfortable with looking at positions from Black's perspective and solving tough tactical problems from that side.

Our classifcation system is quite direct in that we most often tell you, under the "theme column" in the introductions to Chapters One and Three, exactly what pieces and/or Pawns are creating the mate. For instance, Position No. 17 in Chapter One is a classic Rook plus Bishop corridor mate on the 8th rank and we urge you to look at it right now and solve it!

Hint: the solution begins with a **quiet move**, a move that is neither a check nor a capture, which is why quiet moves are often the hardest to find.

Queen support mate simply means that you are mating the enemy King by placing your Queen next to it, with another one of your pieces or Pawns also attacking the mating square which you have just placed your Queen on. An example of this is the following position where, with White to move, the Spanish master Vilardebo missed an opportunity to checkmate one of the world's greatest players, Richard Reti, at the First Chess Olympiad, London 1927.

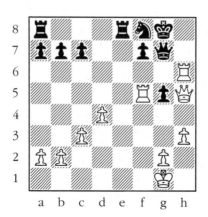

What would you have played? Notice that Black's Queen is what we call **overloaded** in that it has to defend against mates on both h8 and f7. We hope you found the answer: **1. Rh8+!** (a classic *deflection*, making the Queen give up her defense of f7). 1...**Qxh8** forced, **2. Qxf7#.**

A **discovery** is any move by a piece or Pawn which opens a line of fire onto the enemy King, via a rank, file or diagonal, from a piece lurking behind the just moved unit. The most devastating discoveries are usually **double checks**, as in the example below where White mates in three moves.

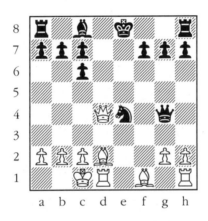

This looks really tough, but at the Paris Tournament of 1878 Maczulsky created a spectacular checkmate against Kolisch by means of a deadly discovered double check: **1. Qd8+!! Kxd8; 2. Bg5+ Kf8; 3. Rd8#.**

Although you may already know what a *pin* is in chess, you may not be sure how pins can be used tactically to force checkmate. We suggest you go immediately to Positions 79 and 80 in Chapter One. In each of these examples, White forces mate in two moves by creating a murderous pin by sacrificing a piece.

Now, we come to what is probably the most difficult tactical concept of all, especially when it is used to force checkmate, namely the "dreaded" zugswang. **Zugswang** basically means "compulsion to move". The losing side must make a move, but would rather not because the only legal moves available cause immediate loss.

Consider the following situation:

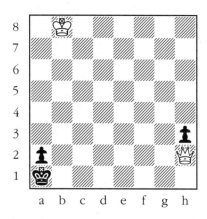

It is White's move. Would you grab the h Pawn or...? We certainly hope not because then the position is theoretically a draw! But, perhaps you noticed that after 1. Qc2!, Black is not only not *stalemated* as he would have been had there been no h Pawn, but is, in fact, in *zugswang*, as his only legal move 1... h2, allows 2. Qc1#.

Finally, you will notice that throughout the book there are an abundance of sacrifices. Particularly evident and exciting are the Queen sacrifices to open lines of attack, to annihilate defenders, to draw off or deflect defenders, or to attract the King to the mating square.

The whole tactical canon of chess is condensed in the challenging mates you will find in this book.

Enjoy.

Fred Wilson & Bruce Alberston,
New York, January 1998

CHAPTER 1

WHITE TO MOVE AND MATE IN TWO

WHITE MATES IN TWO
"White mates in two" indicates that White moves first, Black responds, and White delivers checkmate on his second move. Computer people think of this as three individual moves, or three-ply. Chess folks, accustomed to thinking in move pairs, refer to this as a two-mover. Technically, it's just a move and a half, as Black never gets to make his second move.

ORGANIZATION
The layout of Chapter One is by theme. Typical mating configurations and strategems are grouped together to aid familiarization. Here's what to look for:

Problem Numbers	Theme
1-13	Back rank and other corridor mates
14-27	Rook and Bishop corridors
28-39	Diagonal mates with Queen and Bishop or Rook and Bishop or only a Bishop!
40-48	Bishop and Knight Mates
49-64	Support mates with the Queen
65-73	Knight checkmates
74-78	Pawn mates and promotion
79-92	Pins and discoveries
93-100	Quiet moves and Zugswang

SOLVING HINTS

Since the goal is checkmate and you have only two moves to work with, you'll need to operate with forcing moves. The most forcing moves are also the most violent moves: checks, captures and immediate threats of mate. Also, don't be afraid to sacrifice. Material becomes irrelevant when you're hunting down the enemy King.

Go to it now and get the enemy King.

1.

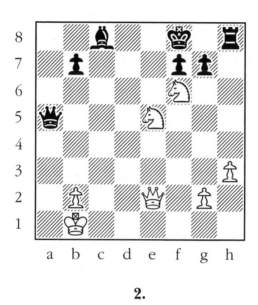

2.

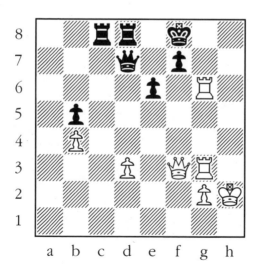

3.

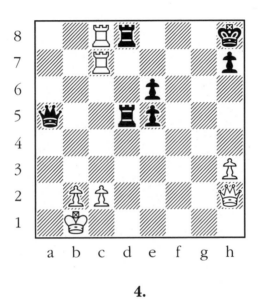

4.

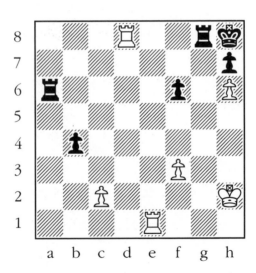

5.

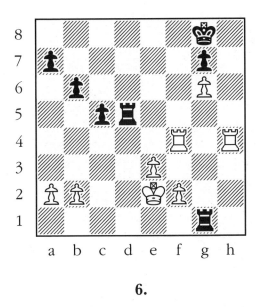

6.

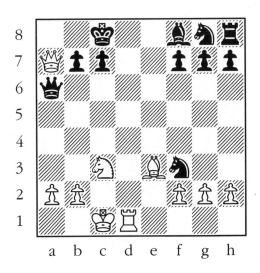

7.

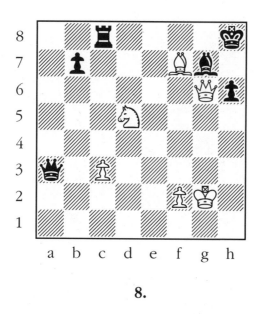

8.

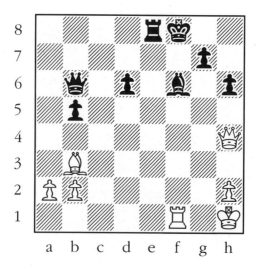

9.

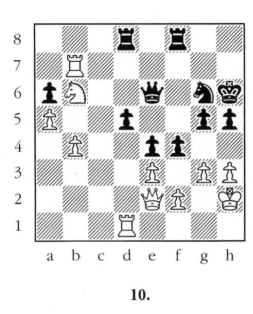

10.

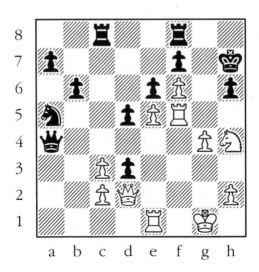

11.

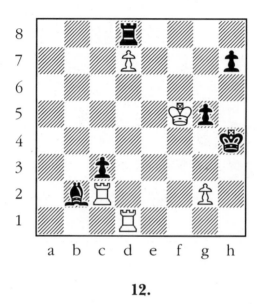

12.

13.

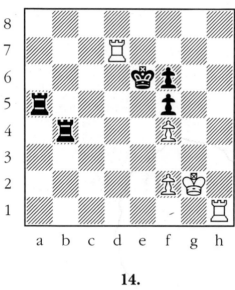

14.

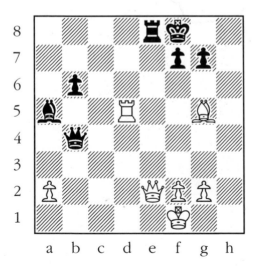

15.

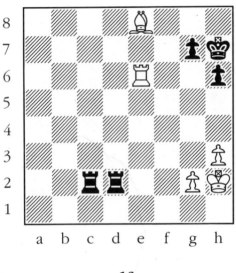

16.

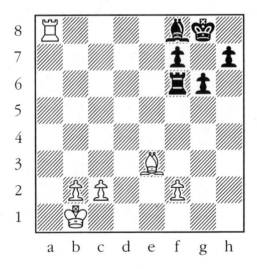

17.

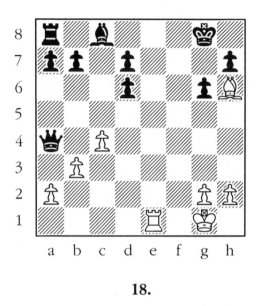

18.

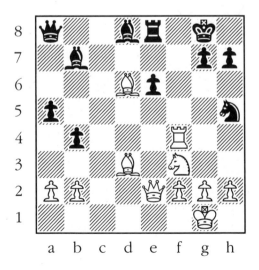

19.

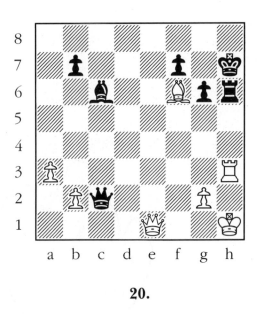

20.

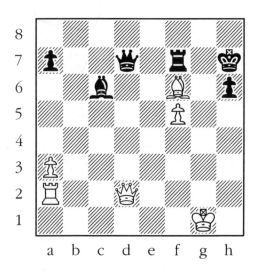

21.

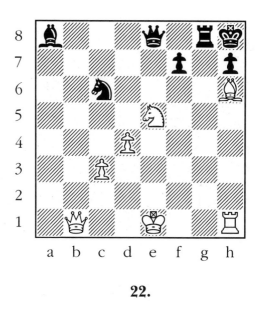

22.

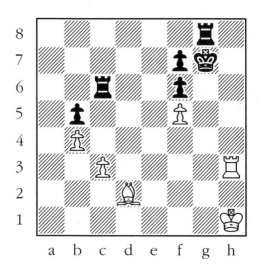

23.

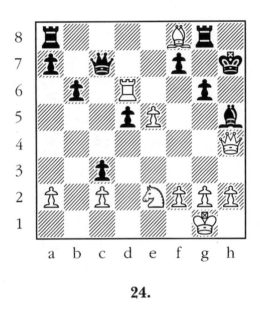

24.

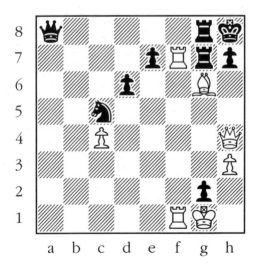

25.

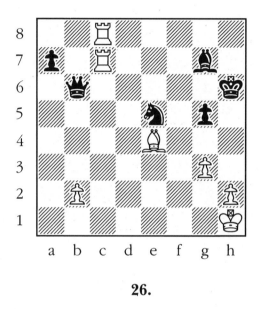

26.

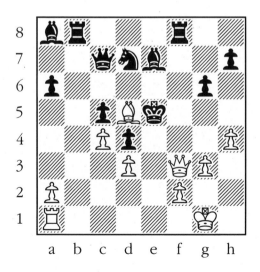

27.

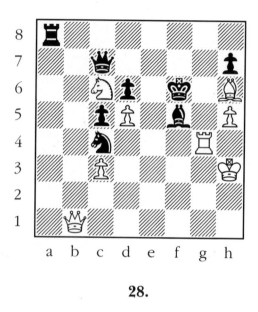

28.

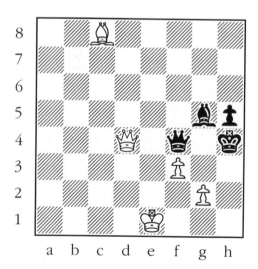

29.

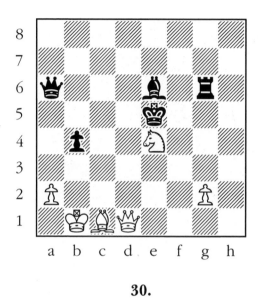

30.

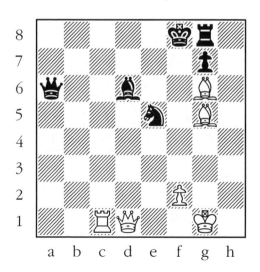

31.

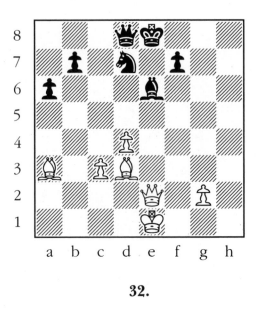

32.

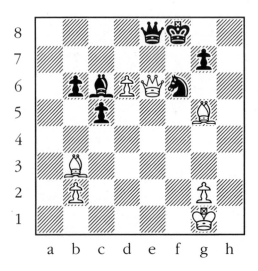

33.

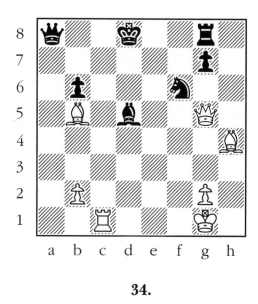

34.

35.

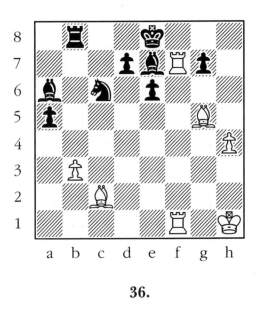

36.

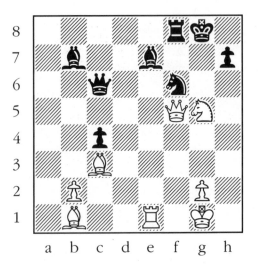

37.

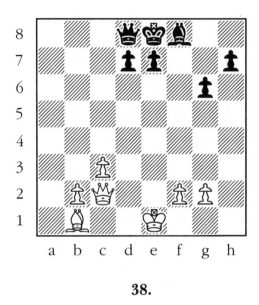

38.

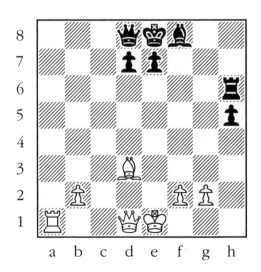

39.

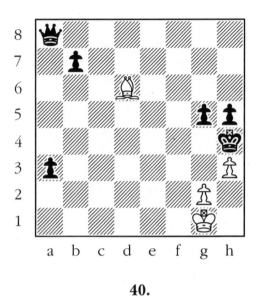

40.

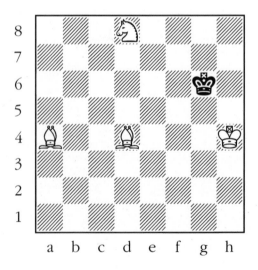

41.

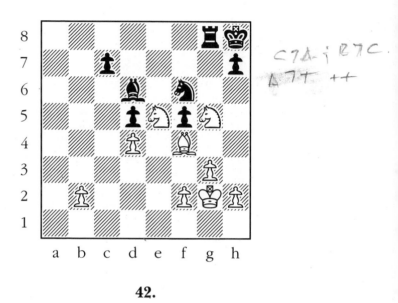

C7A-; R7C.
A7T ++

42.

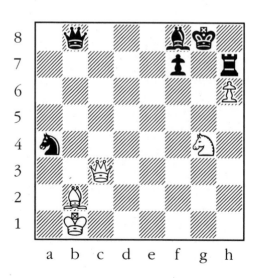

D 8T +; TxD
CGA ++

43.

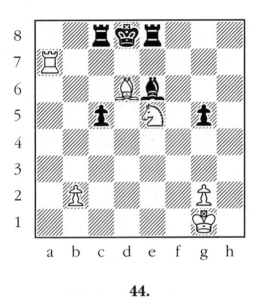

44.

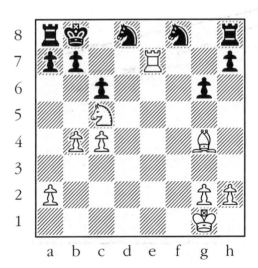

45.

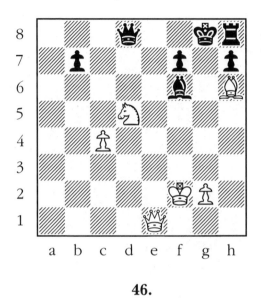

46.

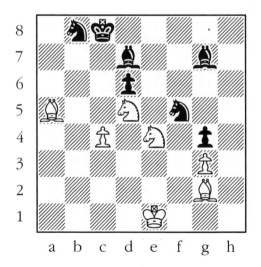

47.

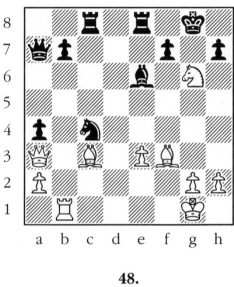

48.

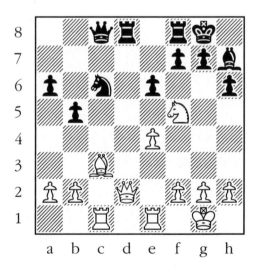

49.

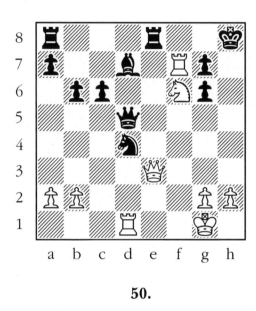

50.

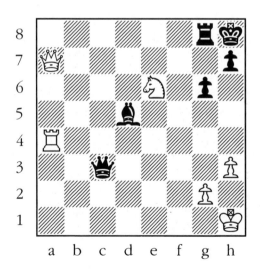

51.

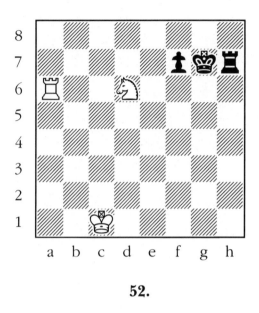

52.

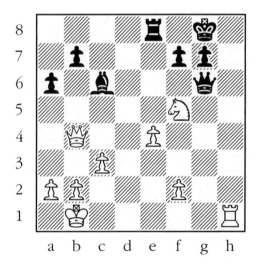

53.

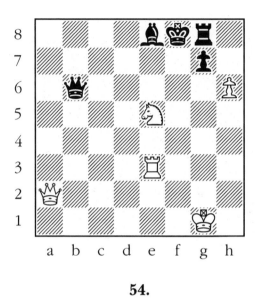

54.

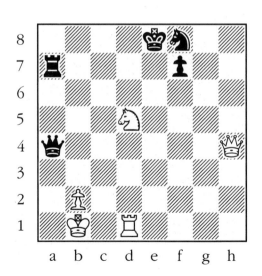

55.

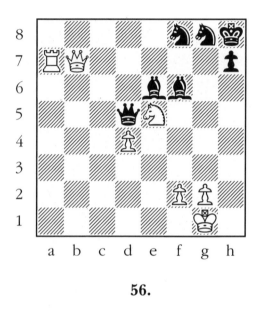

56.

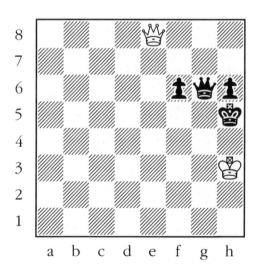

57.

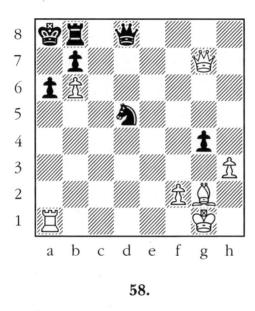

58.

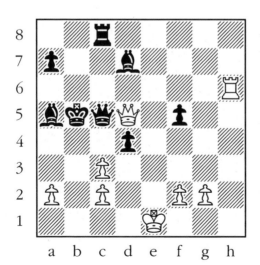

59.

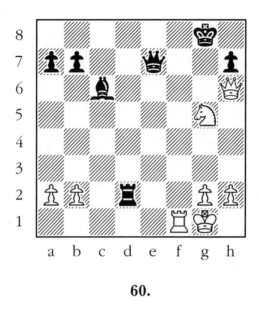

60.

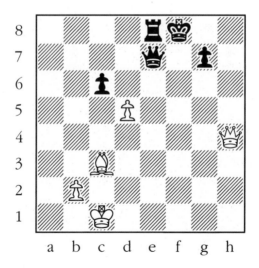

61.

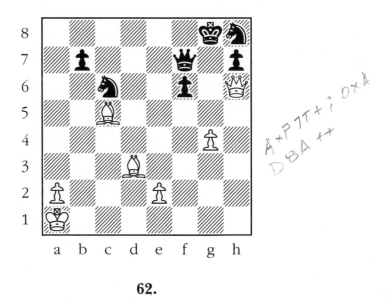

62.

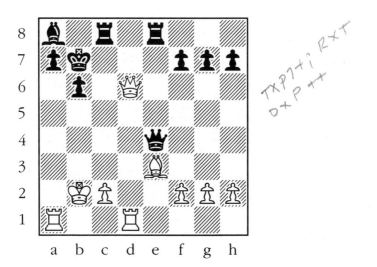

63.

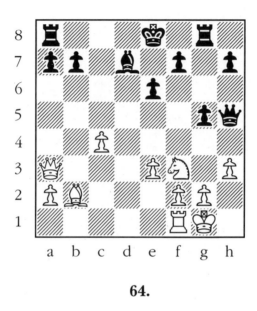

64.

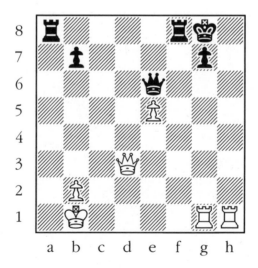

65.

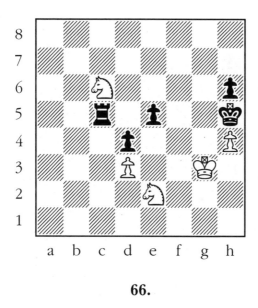

66.

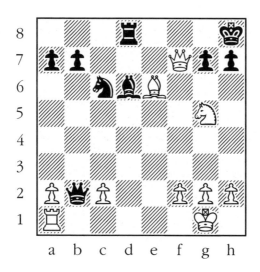

67.

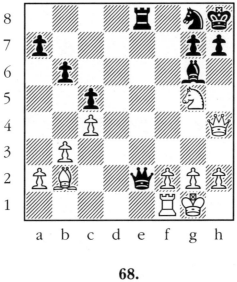

68.

69.

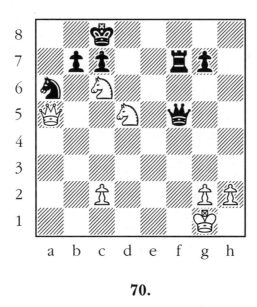

70.

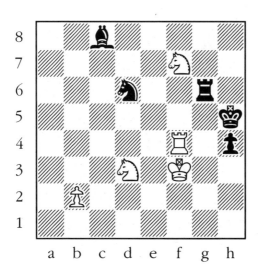

71.

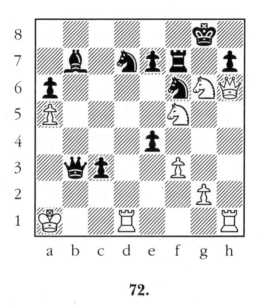

72.

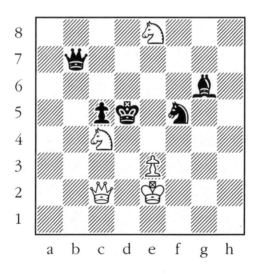

73.

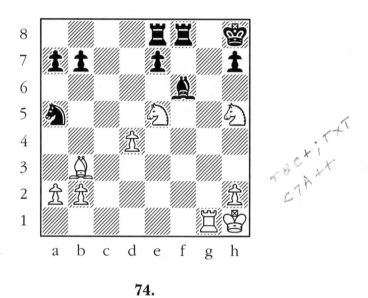

74.

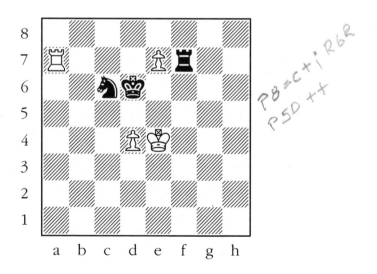

75.

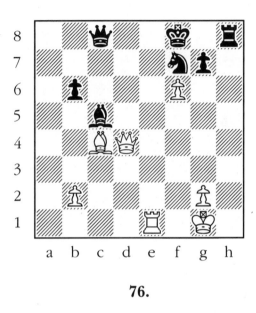

76.

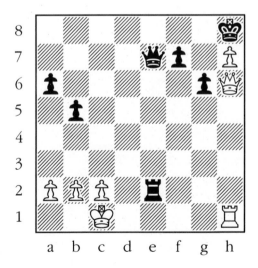

77.

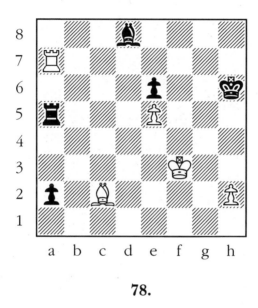

78.

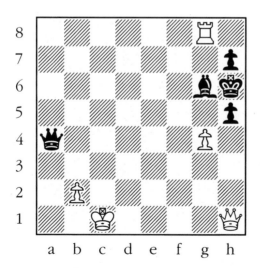

79.

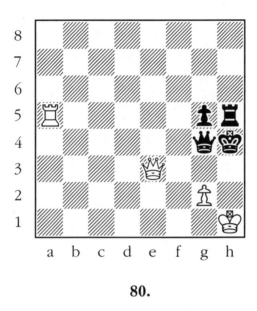

80.

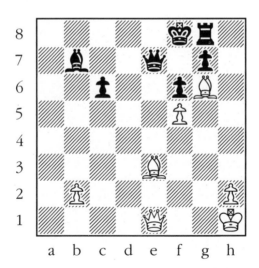

81.

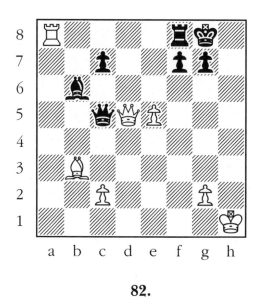

82.

83.

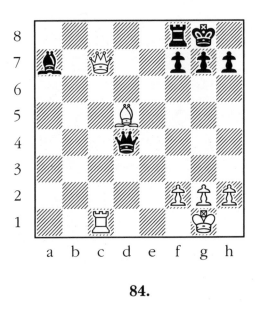

84.

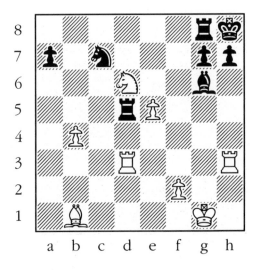

85.

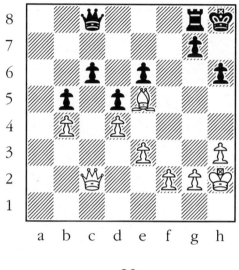

86.

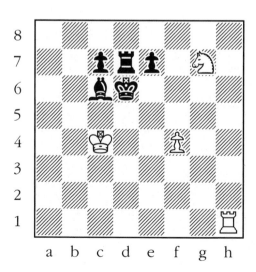

87.

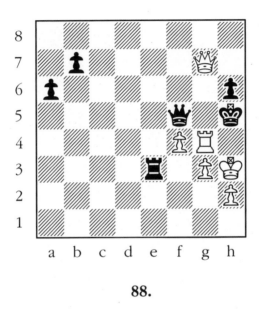

88.

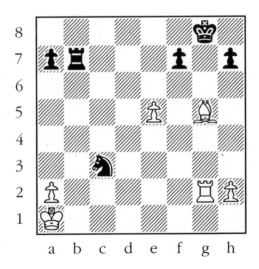

89.

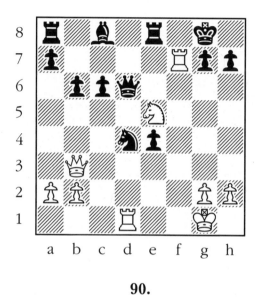

90.

91.

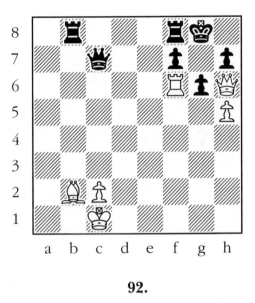

92.

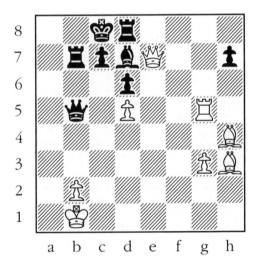

93.

94.

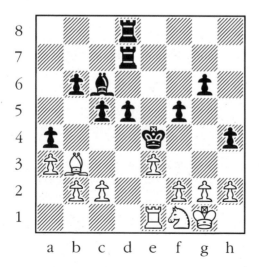

95.

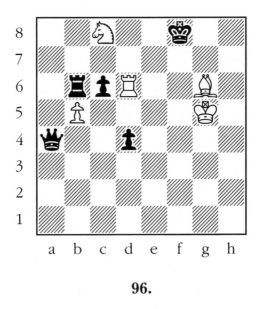

96.

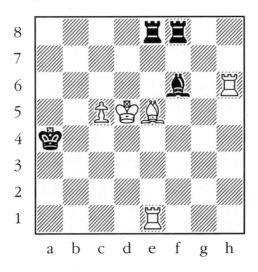

97.

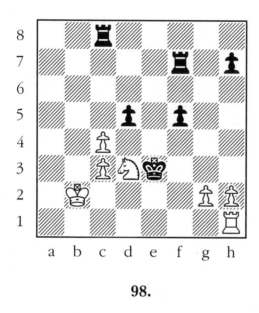

98.

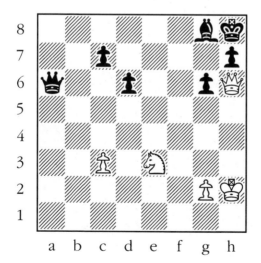

99.

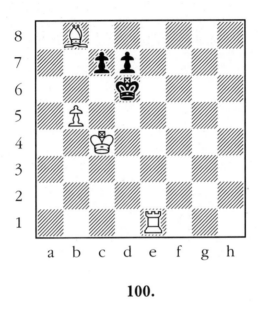

100.

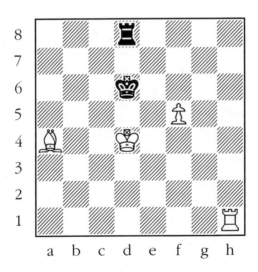

CHAPTER 2

BLACK TO MOVE AND MATE IN TWO

BLACK MATES IN TWO

Here Black gets to make the first move, or the *key move* as it is sometimes called. White replies, and Black administers checkmate on his second move. There's nothing unusual about viewing the position from Black's perspective. In chess games, you'll have the Black pieces half the time. And Black also wins his share of the games.

ORGANIZATION

The mates are organized randomly, deliberately so. You're expected to see your way without any prompting. But here at least, as opposed to an actual game situation, you have the advantage of knowing mate is imminent.

In general, the problems in this section are harder than those in the previous one. More imagination is required and there are more side variations to consider. By this stage, however, most of the patterns should already be familiar, so it's a matter of applying what you already know.

SOLVING HINTS

As in the last chapter, forcing moves are the order of the day. Checks and captures with checks abound. Material sacrifice is by now a commonplace occurance. The idea is to make the position bend to your will. Forcing moves will do it.

Problem #132 comes from our dirty tricks department. You'll need to know two things: the *en passant* capture, and White's last move, b2-b4.

Positions #130 and #140 are composed problems. They are included here more for their curiosity than for anything else. In each, Black places a piece on a square where it can be captured in multiple ways. Each mode of capture weakens the White defense in some fashion, allowing Black to mate. A methodical approach to these mates work best.

You are ready to begin Chapter Two. The objective is the White monarch. Go after him.

101.

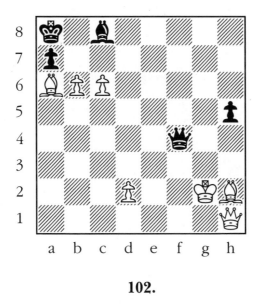

102.

103.

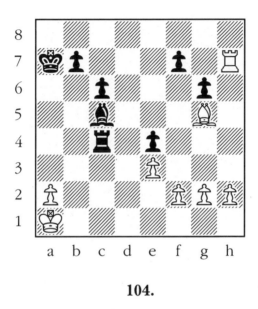

104.

105.

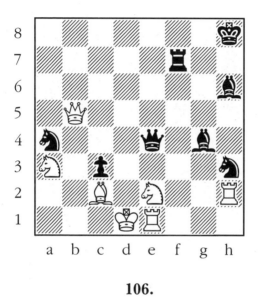

106.

107.

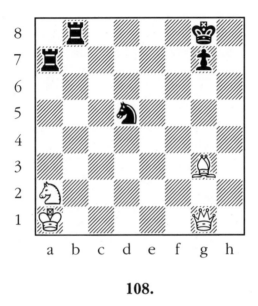

108.

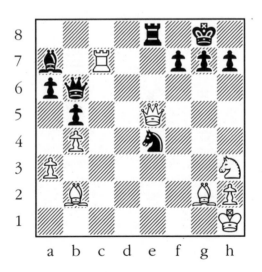

109.

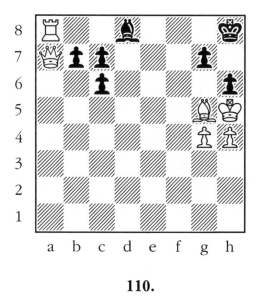

110.

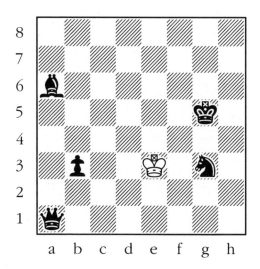

111.

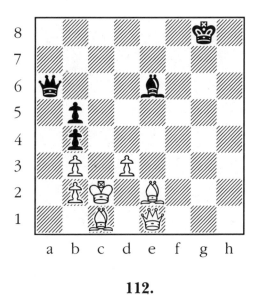

112.

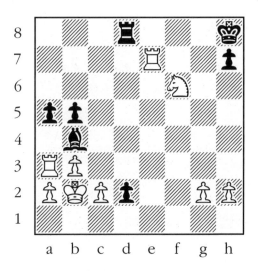

113.

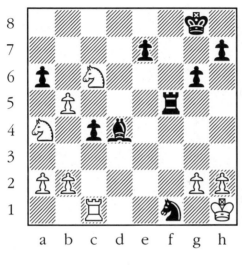

114.

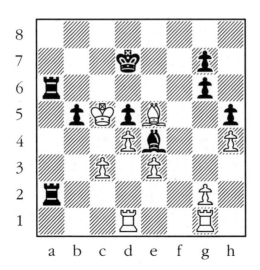

115.

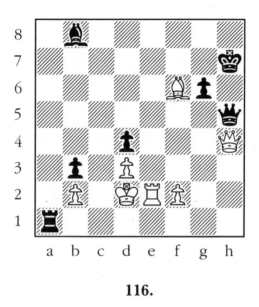

116.

117.

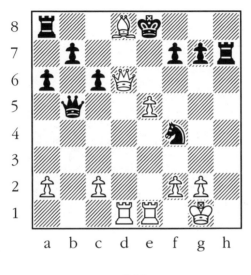

118.

119.

120.

121.

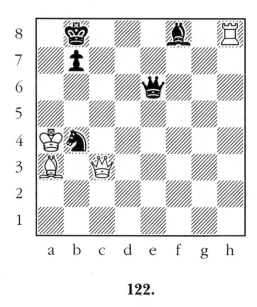

122.

123.

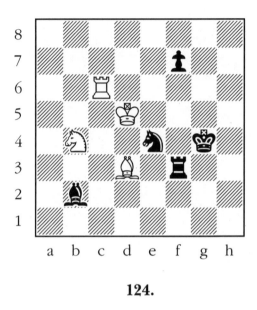

124.

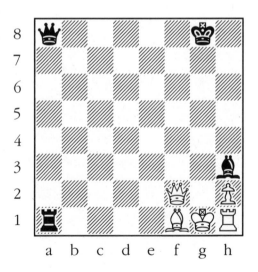

125.

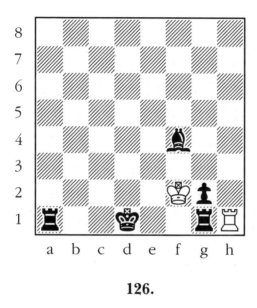

126.

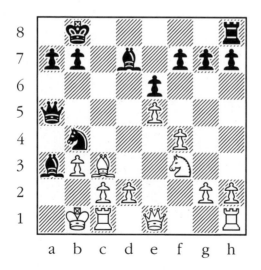

127.

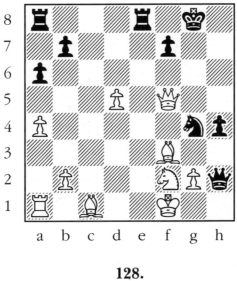

128.

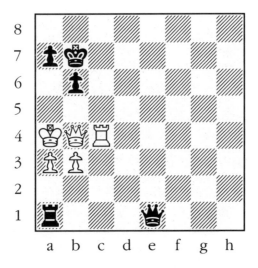

129.

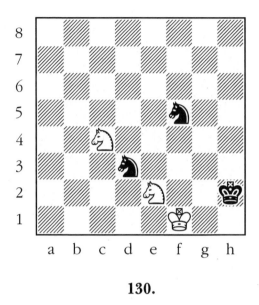

130.

131.

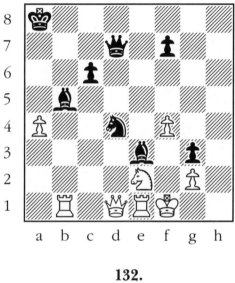

132.

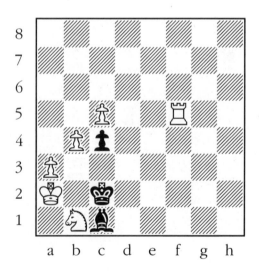

133.

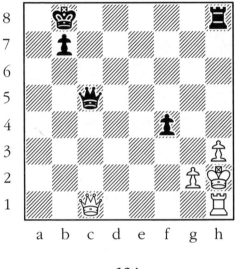

134.

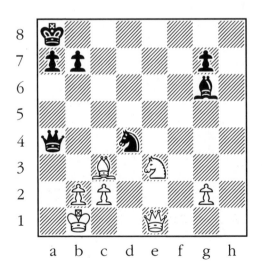

135.

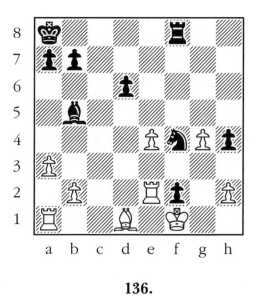

136.

137.

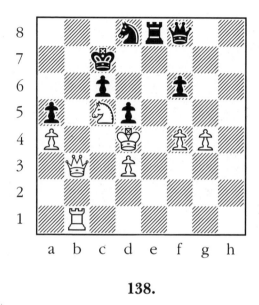

138.

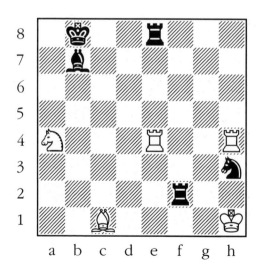

139.

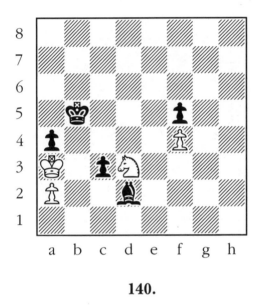

140.

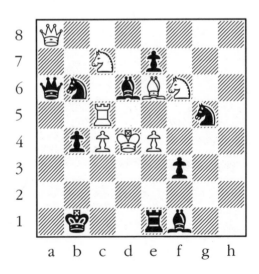

141.

142.

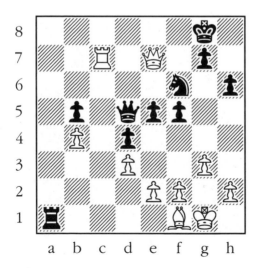

143.

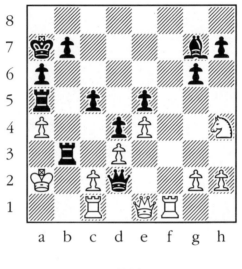

144.

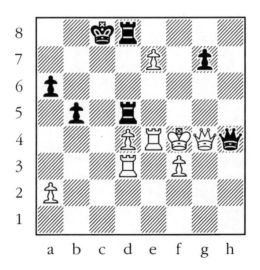

145.

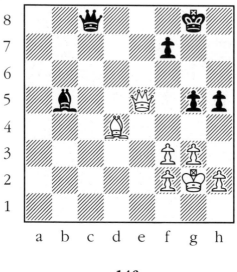

146.

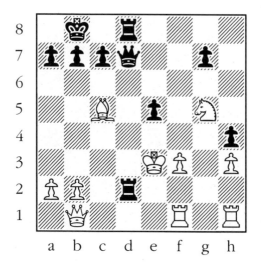

147.

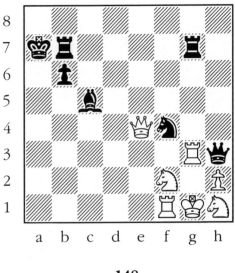

148.

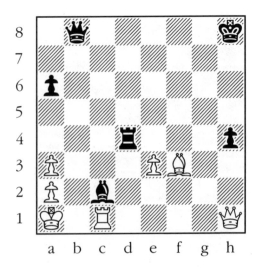

149.

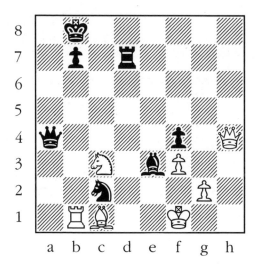

150.

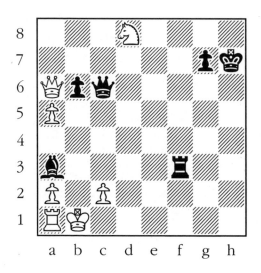

CHAPTER 3

WHITE TO MOVE AND MATE IN THREE

WHITE MATES IN THREE
In this chapter, it is White's turn to initiate the action: White moves, Black moves, White moves, Black moves, White's third move is checkmate. White uses moves one and two to open lines for his pieces, eliminate defenders, take away escape squares from the enemy King – in short, everything necessary to insure that move three is mate.

ORGANIZATION
The fundamental ideas of chess are fairly constant, thus, the catagories in this chapter look pretty much like those in Chapter One. But the numerous ways of implementing those basic ideas is where these mates get interesting.

Problem Numbers	Theme
151-170	Back rank and other corridors
171-177	Rook and Bishop corridors
178-185	Bishop combinations: Q&B; N&B; 2 Bs.
186-193	Rook and Knight Mates
194-212	Queen support mates
213-220	Knight mates
221-228	Promotion and pawn mates
229-243	Pins and discoveries
244-250	Quiet moves and Zugswang

SOLVING HINTS
We've advanced from the two mover to the three mover. In many instances, this is merely a lengthening of the mating process, a one move extension of a two move idea. Number 160 is a case in

point. At its core, #160 is essentially the same as the two-mover, #15. But just as often, there is an extra dimension, a concept that cannot be carried out in less than three moves.

Your task then: extend and conceptualize to mate.

151.

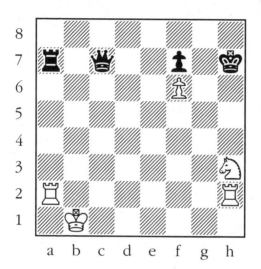

C 1 1 + ; R 1 C
T D 2 C + ; R 1 A
T 2 7 8 T + +

152.

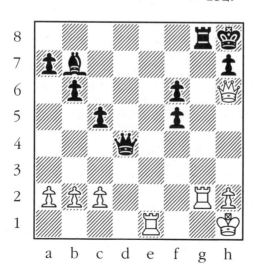

153.

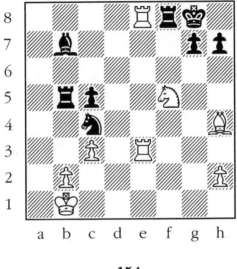

154.

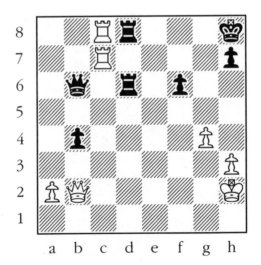

155.

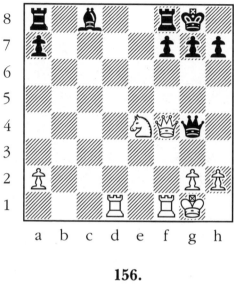

156.

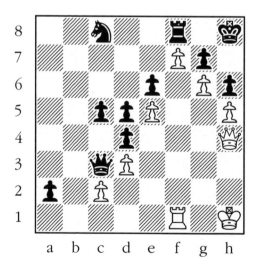

157.

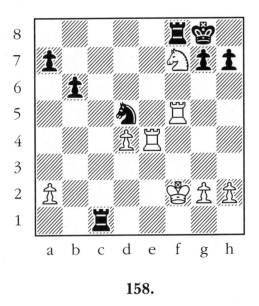

158.

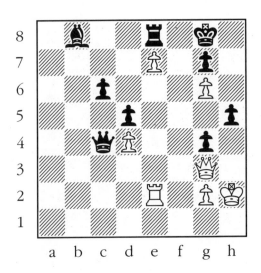

159.

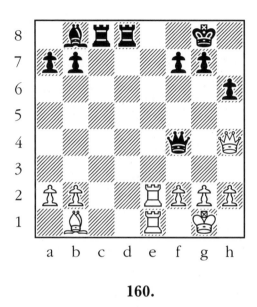

160.

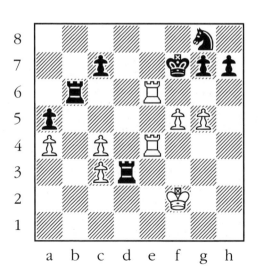

161.

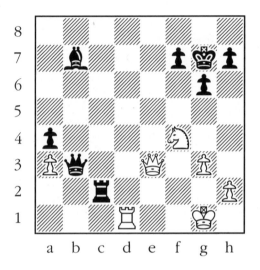

162.

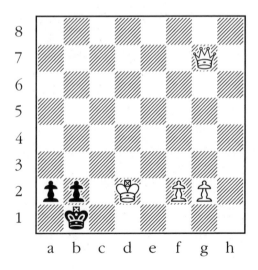

163.

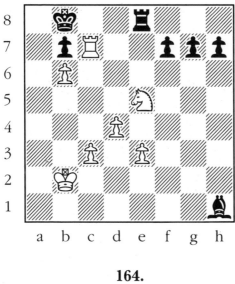

164.

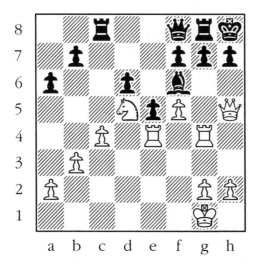

165.

166.

167.

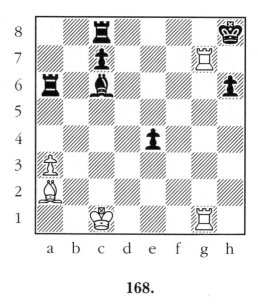

168.

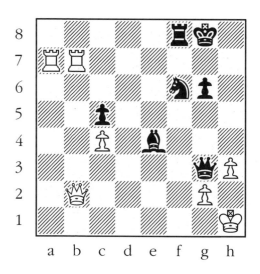

169.

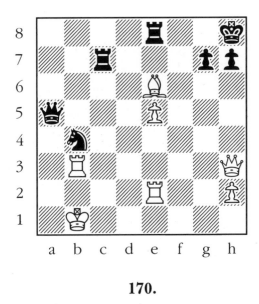

170.

171.

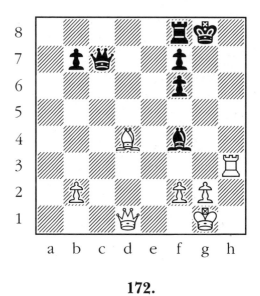

172.

173.

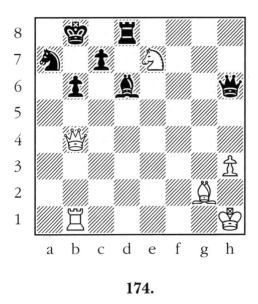

174.

175.

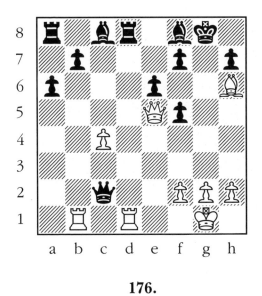

176.

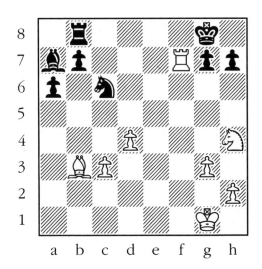

177.

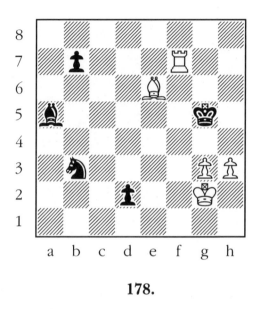

178.

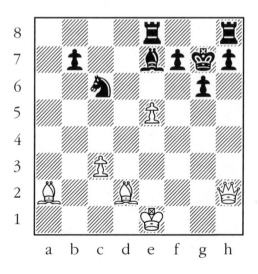

179.

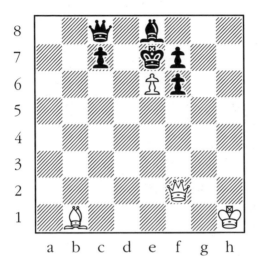

180.

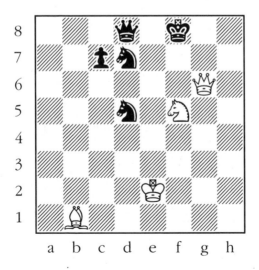

181.

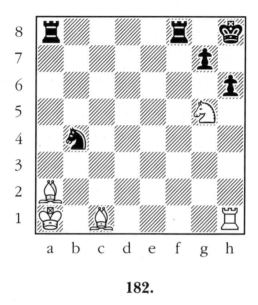

182.

183.

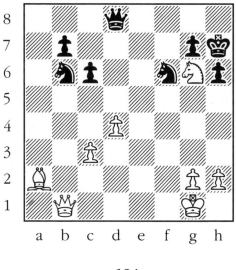

184.

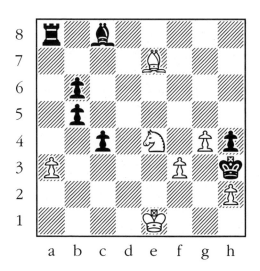

185.

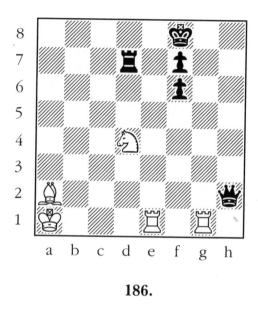

186.

187.

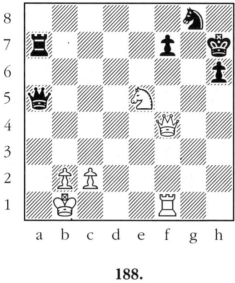

188.

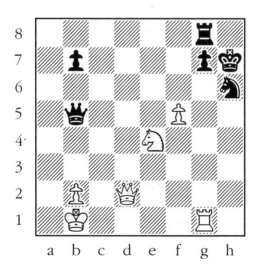

189.

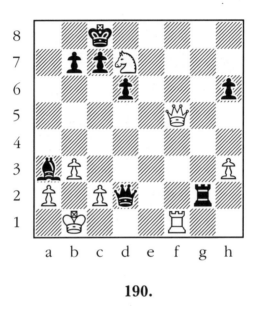

190.

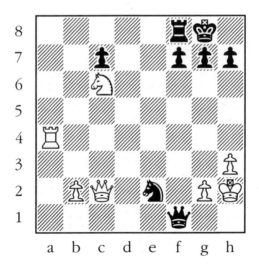

191.

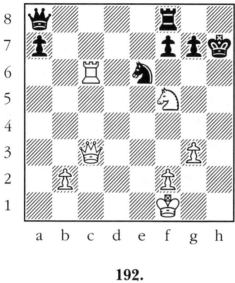

192.

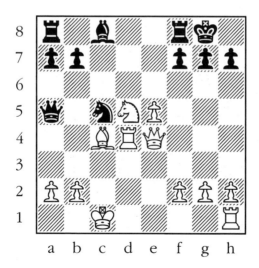

193.

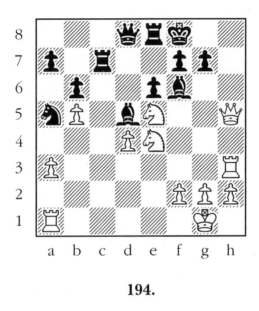

194.

195.

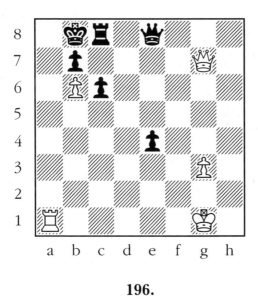

196.

197.

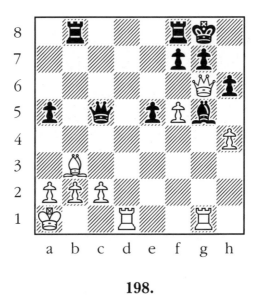

198.

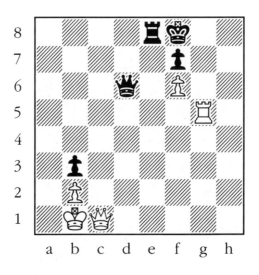

199.

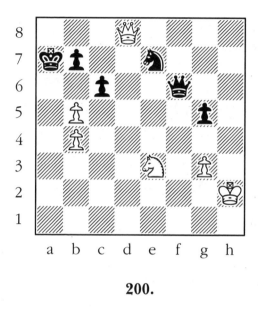

200.

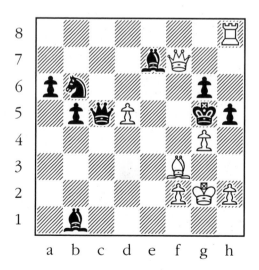

201.

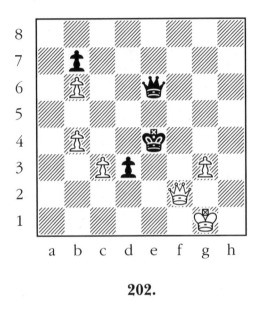

202.

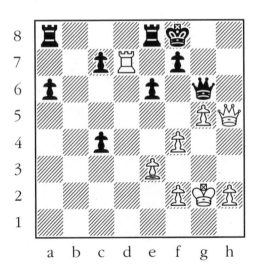

203.

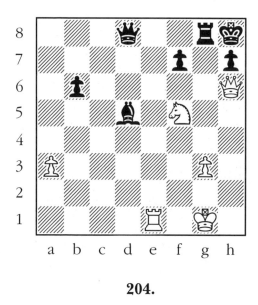

204.

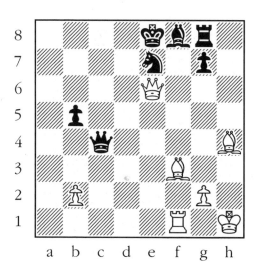

205.

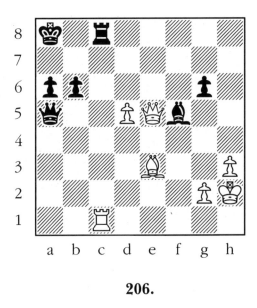

206.

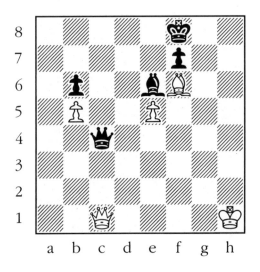

207.

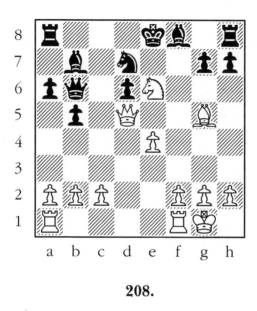

208.

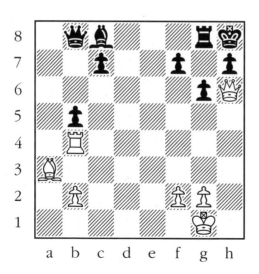

209.

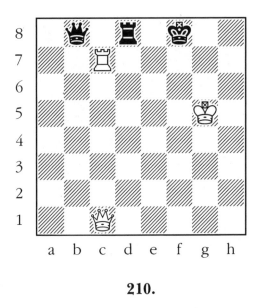

210.

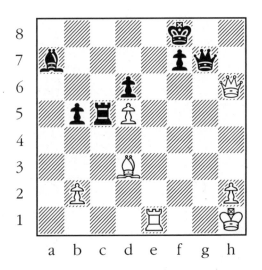

211.

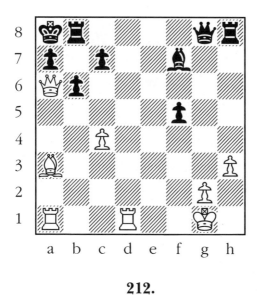

212.

213.

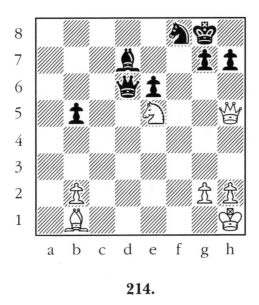

214.

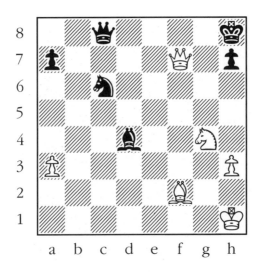

215.

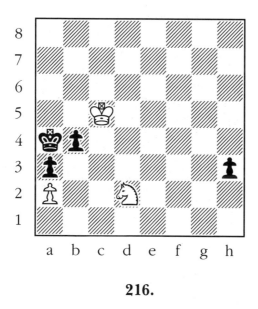

216.

217.

218.

219.

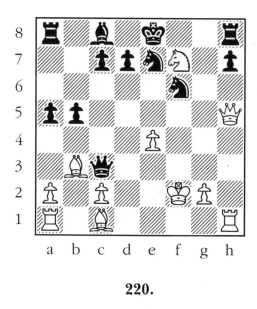

220.

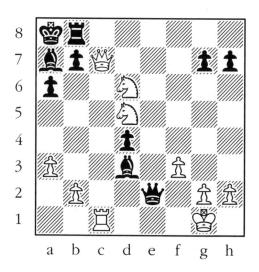

221.

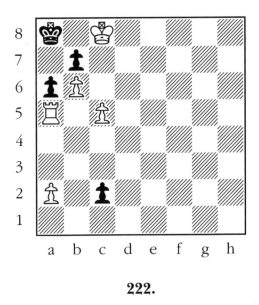

222.

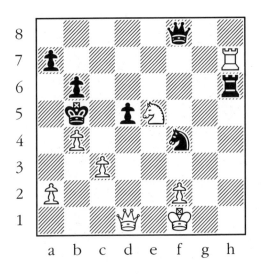

223.

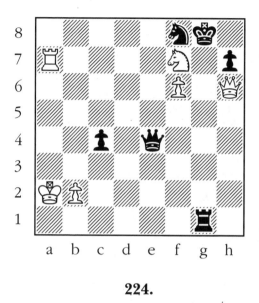

224.

225.

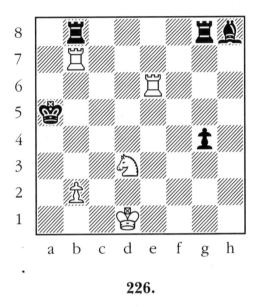

226.

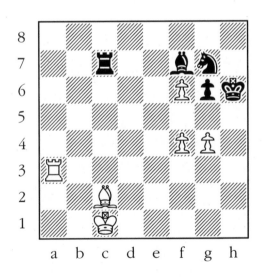

227.

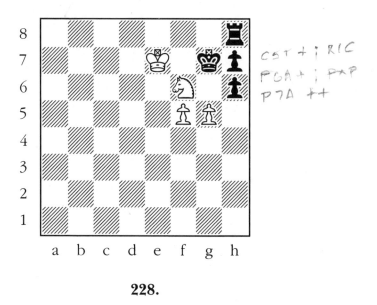

CST + ; RIC
PSA + ; PAP
P7A ++

228.

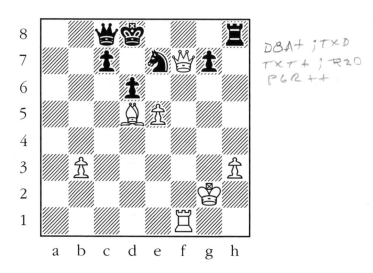

DBA+ ; TXD
TXT+ ; R2D
P6R ++

229.

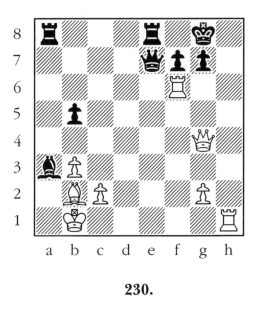

230.

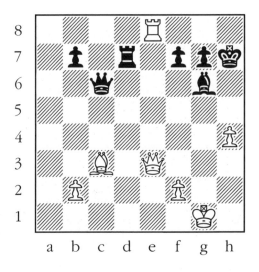

231.

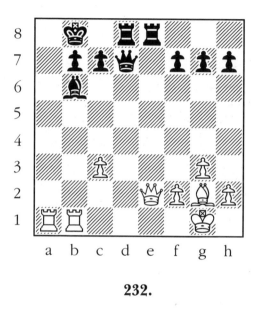

232.

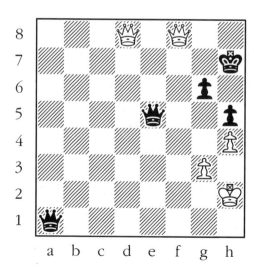

233.

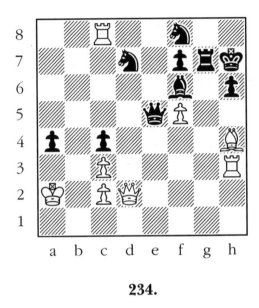

234.

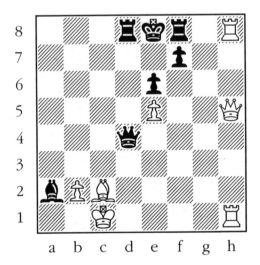

235.

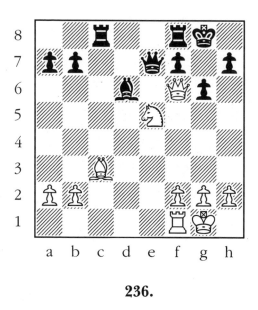

236.

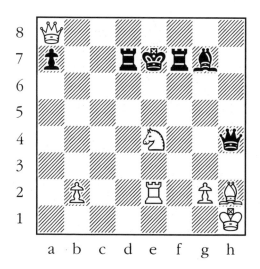

237.

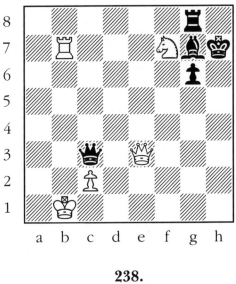

238.

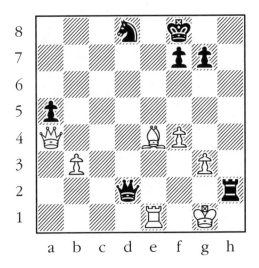

239.

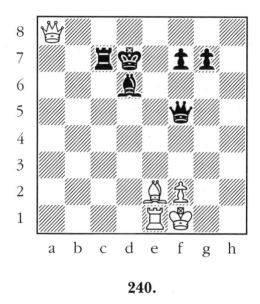

240.

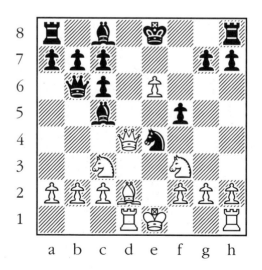

241.

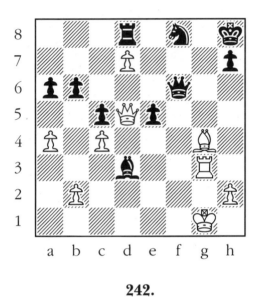

242.

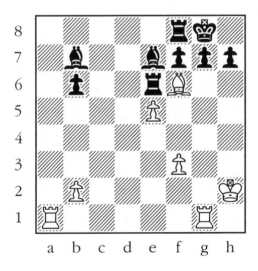

243.

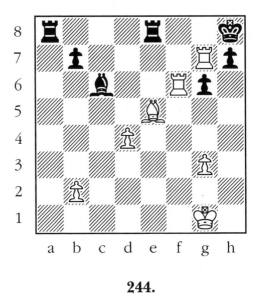

244.

245.

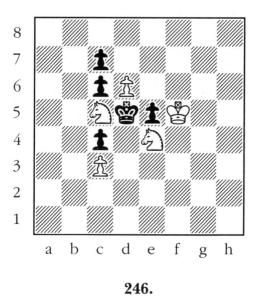

246.

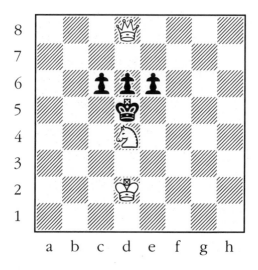

247.

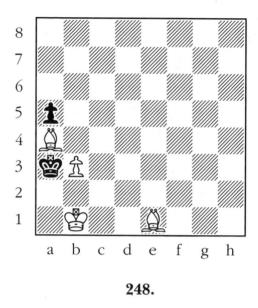

248.

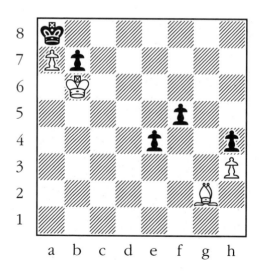

249.

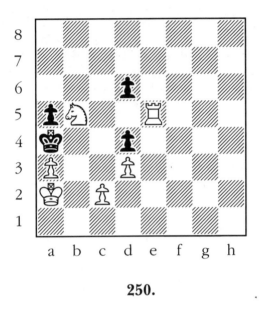

250.

CHAPTER 4

BLACK TO MOVE AND MATE IN THREE

BLACK MATES IN THREE
It's Black's turn again. The sequence is Black, White, Black, White, Black. This third Black move is mate.

The problems in this section are harder than those in the preceding chapter. Black's job always seems to be tougher than White's due to White's inherent advantage in going first. More ingenuity is required, more calculation as well. But you should be up to the task.

ORGANIZATION
The positions have been randomized for the greatest challenges.

SOLVING HINTS
The time has come to give away the biggest secret of all: the answers are in the back of the book. So, if you get stuck on a mate, look it up. Then let some time go by, come back, and try again.

251.

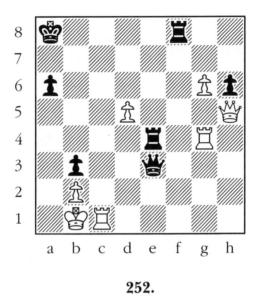

252.

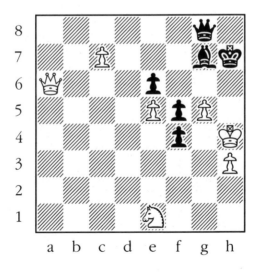

253.

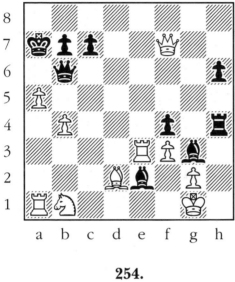

254.

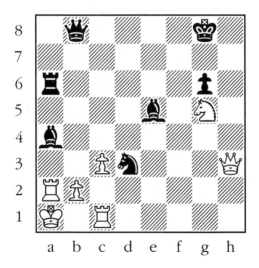

255.

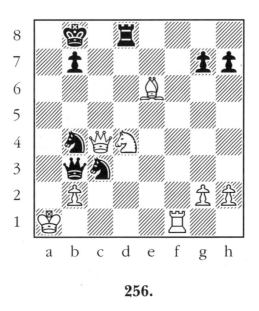

256.

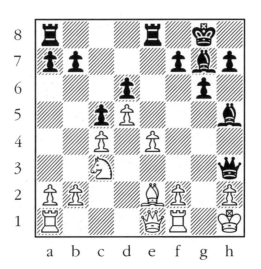

257.

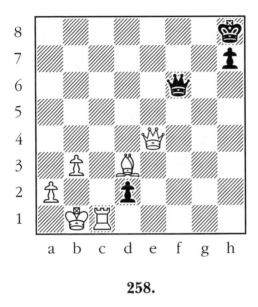

258.

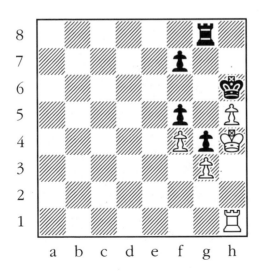

259.

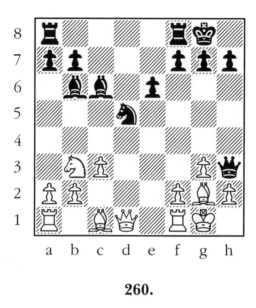

260.

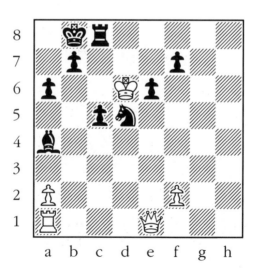

261.

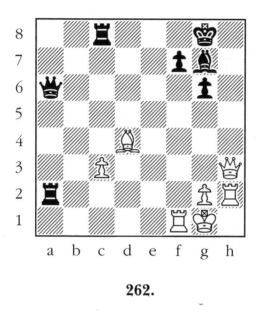

262.

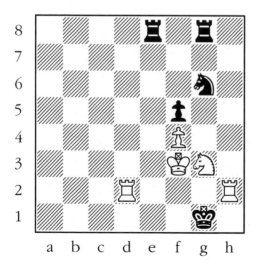

263.

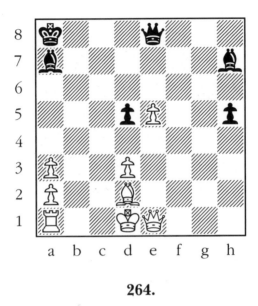

264.

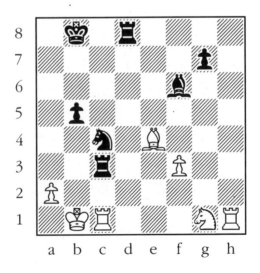

265.

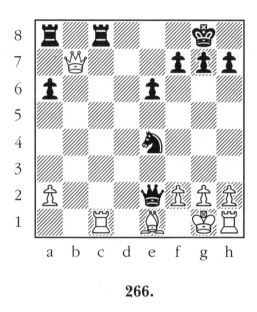

266.

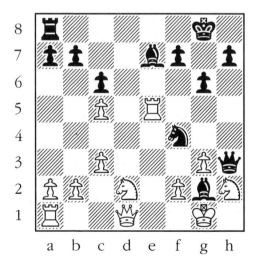

267.

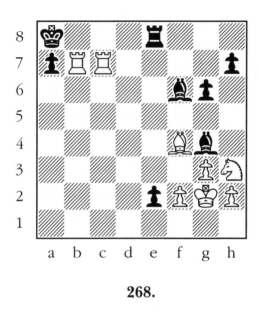

268.

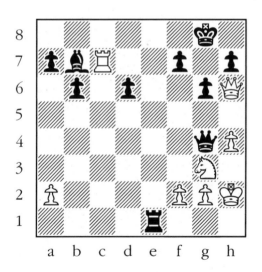

269.

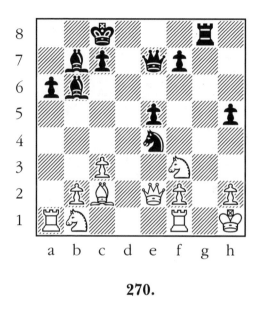

270.

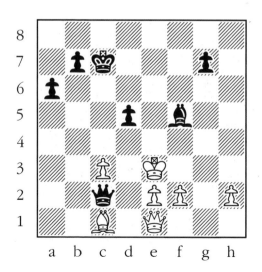

271.

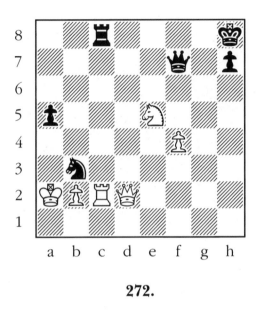

272.

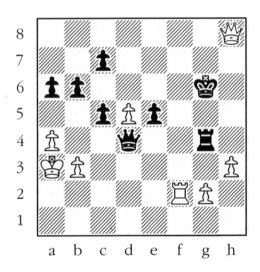

273.

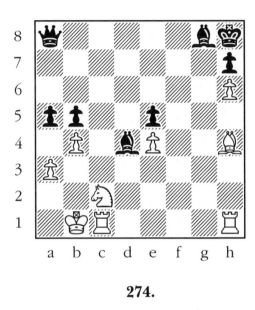

274.

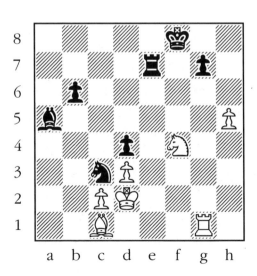

275.

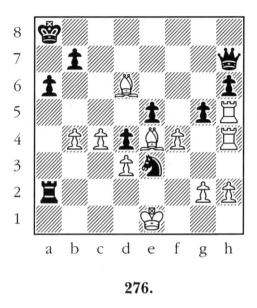

276.

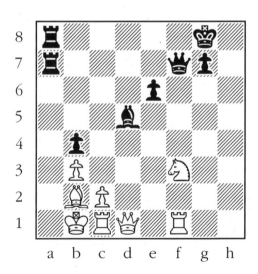

277.

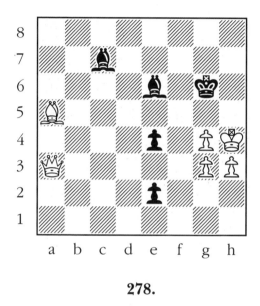

278.

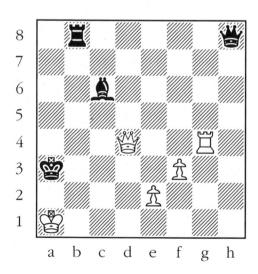

279.

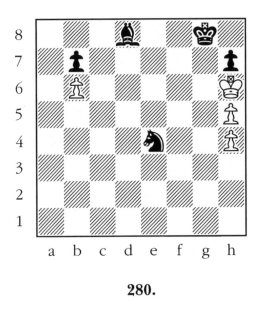

280.

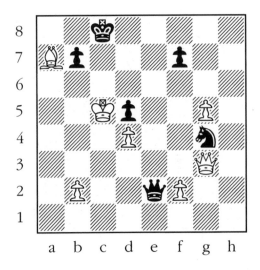

281.

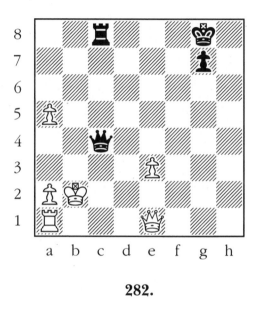

282.

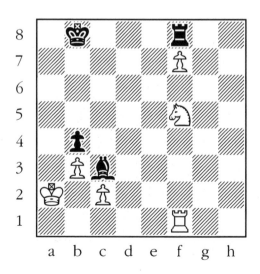

283.

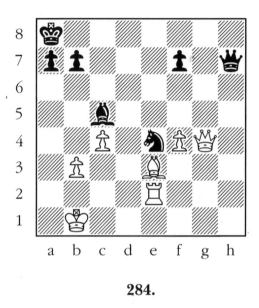

284.

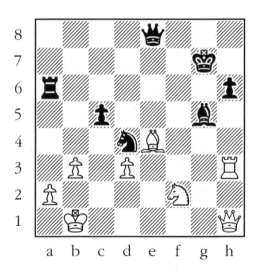

285.

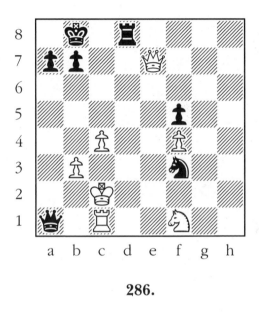

286.

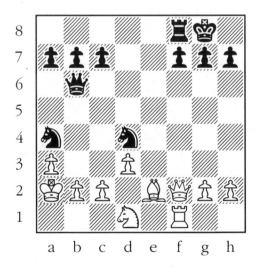

287.

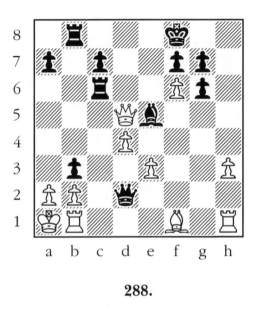

288.

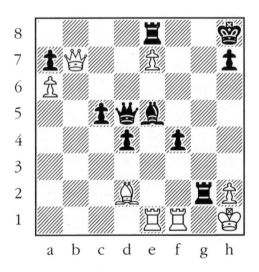

289.

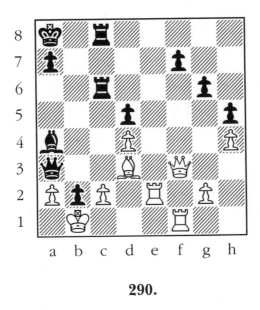

290.

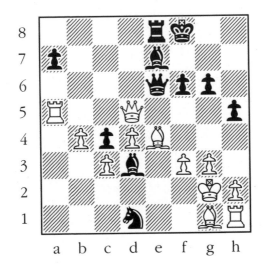

291.

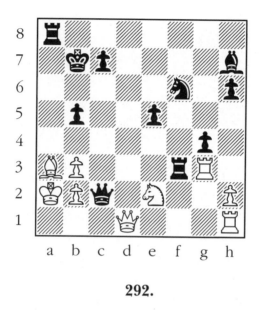

292.

293.

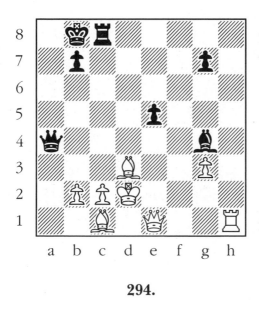

294.

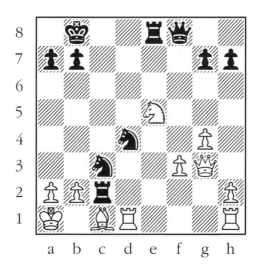

295.

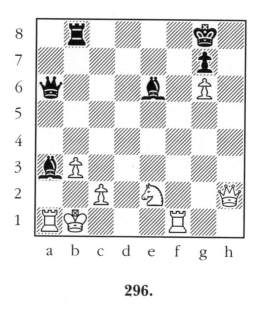

296.

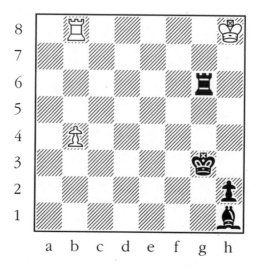

297.

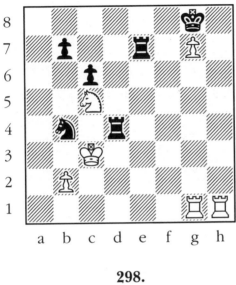

298.

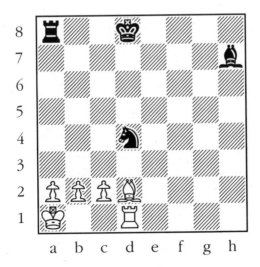

299.

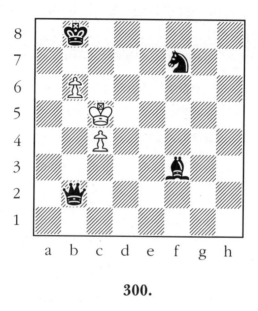

300.

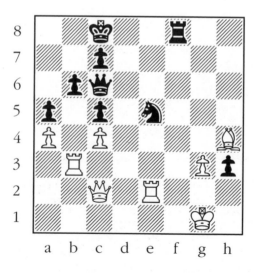

CHAPTER 5

WHITE TO MOVE AND MATE IN FOUR

WHITE MATES IN FOUR

You are about to enter the exalted realm of the four mover. White goes first, Black responds, you know the rest. Mate comes with White's fourth move.

Battle-hardened by your journey through the tricky mates in this book, you are no doubt expecting a reward for all your noble efforts. The big payoff will come when you apply what you've learned to your own games. It's either that or wait for our next book.

Meanwhile, we offer a few tasty morsels for your last challenges.

301.

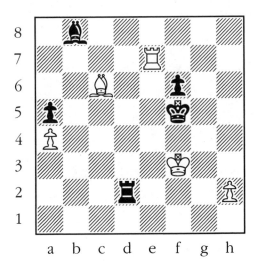

302.

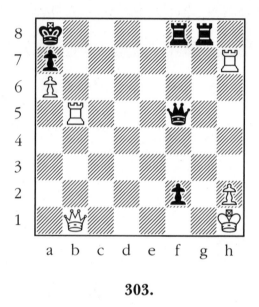

303.

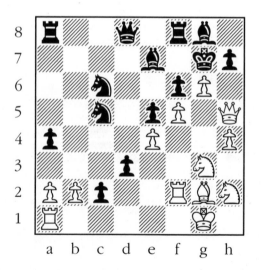

SOLUTIONS

#1. **1. Ng6+ fxg6 2. Qe8#**

#2. **1. Qf6** *and* **2. Rg8#**

#3. **1. Qxe5+**
    (A) 1...Kg7 2. Qg7#
    (B) 1...Rxe5 2. Rxd8#

#4. **1. R1e8** (*threatens* **2. Rxg8#**)
    1...Rxe8 2. Rxe8#

#5. **1. Rh8+ Kxh8 2. Rf8#**

#6. **1. Qb8+ Kxb8 2. Rd8#**

#7. **1. Nf6** (*threatens* **2. Qh7#**)
    1...Bxf6 2. Qxh6#

#8. **1. Rxf6+**
    (A) 1...gxf6 2. Qxf6#
    (B) 1...Ke7 2. Rf7#
    Double check and mate.

#9. **1. Qxh5+ Kxh5 2. Rh7#**

#10. **1. Qxh6+ (A) 1...Kg8 2. Rg5#**
    (B) 1...Kxh6 2. Rh5#

#11. **1. Rh1+ Kg3 2. Rh3#**

#12. **1. Ne5+ Kxd4 2. Rd2#**

#13. **1. Rhh7** *and* **2. Rhe7#**

#14. **1. Qxe8 Kxe8 2. Rd8#**

#15. **1. Bg6+ Kg8 2. Re8#**

#16. **1. Bh6** *and* **2. Rxf8#**

#17. **1. Rf1** *and* **2. Rf8#**

#18. **1. Qxe6+**
    (A) 1...Kh8 2. Qxe8#
    (B) 1...Rxe6 2. Rf8#

#19. **1. Rxh6+**
    (A) 1...Kxh6 2. Qh4#
    (B) 1...Kg8 2. Rh8#

#20. **1. Qxh6+**
    (A) 1...Kg8 2. Qh8#
    (B) 1...Kxh6 2. Rh2#

#21. **1. Qxh7+ Kxh7 2. Bf8#**

#22. **1. Bh6+ Kh7 2. Bf8#**

#23. **1. Qxh5+ gxh5 2. Rh6#**

#24. **1. Qxh7+ Rxh7 2.Rxh7#**

#25. **1. Rh8+ Bxh8 2. Rh7#**

#26. **1. Re1+ Kd6 2. Re6#**

#27. **1. Qxf5+ Kxf5 2. Rf4#**

#28. **1. g3+ Kxg3 2. Qf2#**

#29. **1. Bb2+ Kxe4 2. Qf3#**

#30. **1. Rc8+ Qxc8 2. Qxd6#**

#31. **1. Qxe6+**
 (A) 1...Qe7 2. Qxe7#
 (B) 1...fxe6 2. Bg6#

#32. **1. Qxe6+**
 (A) 1...Qf7 2. Qxf7#
 (B) 1...gxf6 2. Bh6#

#33. **1. Qxf6+ gxf6 2. Bxf6#**

#34. **1. Bxf7+ Ke7 2. Bg5#**

#35. **1. Rf8+ Bxf8 2. Bg6#**

#36. **1. Qxh7+ Nxh7 2. Bxh7#**

#37. **1. Qxg6+ hxg6 2. Bxg6#**

#38. **1. Qxh5+ Rxh5 2. Bg6#**

#39. **1. Kh2** (*threatens* **2. g3#**)
 1...g4 2. Be7#

#40. **1. Bc2+ Kh6 2. Nf7#**

#41. **1. Ngf7+ Kg7 2. Bh6#**

#42. **1. Qh8+ Rxh8 2. Nf6#**

#43. **1. Rd7+ Bxd7 2. Nf7#**

#44. **1. Rxb7+ Nxb7 2. Na6#**

#45. **1. Qe8+ Qxe8 2. Nxf6#**

#46. **1. Nxd6+ Nxd6 2. Ne7#**

#47. **1. Qf8+ Rxf8 2. Ne7#**

#48. **1. Qxh6** (*threatens* **2. Qxg7#**).
 1...gxh6 2. Nxh6#

#49. **1. Qh6+ gxh6 2. Rh7#**

#50. **1. Qxh7+ Kxh7 2. Rh4#**

#51. **1. Nf5+ Kf8 2. Ra8#**
 Anastasia's Mate

#52. **1. Qf8+**
 (A) 1...Rxf8 2. Ne7#
 (B) 1...Kxf8 2. Rh8#

#53. **1. Qf7+ Bxf7 2. Nd7#**

#54. **1. Qe7+ Rxe7 2. Nf6#**

#55. **1. Qxh7+ Nxh7 2. Ng6#**

#56. **1. Qe2+ Kg5 2. Qg4#**

#57. **1. Rxa6+ bxa6 2. Qa7#**

#58. **1. a4+ Kxa4 2. Qb3#**

#59. **1. Rf8+ Qxf8 2. Qxh7#**

#60. **1. Qh8+ Kf7 2. Qxg7#**

#61. **1. Bxh7+ Qxh7 2. Qf8#**

#62. **1. Rxa7+ Kxa7 2. Qxb6#**

#63. **1. Bf6** *and* **2. Qe7#**

#64. **1. Rxg7+ Kxg7 2. Qh7#**

#65. **1. Nxe5 Rxe5 2. Nf4#**

#66. **1. Qg8+ Rxg8 2. Nf7#**
The old Smothered Mate

#67. **1. Qxh7+ Bxh7 2. Nf7#**

#68. **1. Qxb8+ Qxb8 2. Nb6#**

#69. **1. Qxc7+ Rxc7 2. Nb6#**

#70. **1. Rf5+ (A) 1...Rg5 2. Rxg5#**
(B) 1...N(B)xf5 2. Nf4#

#71. **1. Qg7+ Rxg7 2. Nh6#**

#72. **1. Qe4+ Kxe4 2. Nf6#**

#73. **1. Rg8+ Rxg8 2. Nf7#**

#74. **1. e8/N+ Ke6 2. d5#**

#75. **1. fxg7+ Kg8 2. gxh8/Q#**
Also a pin mate, as the f7 - Knight cannot capture.

#76. **1. Qg7+ Kxg7 2. h8/Q#**

#77. **1. Rh7+ Kg5 2. h4#**

#78. **1. Qxh5+ Bxh5 2. g5#**

#79. **1. Ra4 Qxa4 2. Qh3#**

#80. **1. Bc5** *(threatens 2. B(Q)xe7#)*
1...Qxc5 2. Qe8#

#81. **1. Qxf7+ Kh7 2. Qh5#**

#82. **1. Qxh6+ Kg8 2. Q(R)xg7#**

#83. **1. Qxf7+**
(A) 1...Kh8 2. Qxf8#
(B) 1...Rxf7 2. Rc8#

#84. **1. Rxh7+ (A) 1...Bxh7 2. Nf7#**
(B) 1....Kxh7 2. Rh3#

#85. **1. Qg6** *(threatens 2. Qxh6#)*
1...Rf8 2. Qxg7#

#86. **1. Rh6+ e6 2. Nf5#**

#87. **1. Qg6+ Qxg6 2. Rh4#**

#88. **1. Be7+ Kh8 2. Bf6#**

#89. **1. Rf8+ Kxf8 2. Qf7#**

#90. **1. Qh7+ Kxh7 2. Bf7#**

#91. **1. Qg7+ Kxg7 2. Rxg6#**

#92. **1. Qxd8+ Kxd8 2. Rg8#**

#93. **1. c4 Ka5 2. Qa7#**
The en passent capture, 1...bxc3, is illegal, as the b4 pawn is pinned.

#94. **1. f4** *and* **2. Nd2#**

#95. **1. Kh6** *and* **2. Rd8#**
Not 1. Kf6? cxb5! and the d6-Rook is pinned.

#96. **1. Kc4** (*threatens* **2. Ra1#**)
    1...Bxe5 2. Ra6#

#97. **1. Kc2** *and* **2. Re1#**

#98. **1. Nf5** (*threatens* **2. Qg7#**)
    1...gxf5 2.Qf6#

#99. **1. Ba7 c6 2. Bb8#**
    The Switchback theme.

#100. **1. Rh7** *and* **2. R(x)d7#**
    Black is in zugswang and his rook has to give up control of d7.

#101. **1...Bh3+ (A) 2. Kxh3 Qg4#**
    (B) 2. Kg1 Qd4#

#102. **1...Qh6+ (A) 2. Kxh6 Bd2#**
    (B) 2. Bxh6 Bd8#
    (C) 2 Kh4 Be1#

#103. **1...Ba3** *and* **2...Rc1#**

#104. **1...Bxf5** (*threatening* **2...Rh3#**)
    2. Rxf5 R7g4#

#105. **1...Qxe2**
    (A) 2. Rexe2 Rf1#
    (B) 2. Rhxe2 Nf2#
    (C) 2. Qxe2 Nb2#

#106. **1...Bd5+** *and* **2...Qe3#**

#107. **1...Nc3 (A) 2. Bxb8 Rxa2#**
    (B) 2. Qxa7 Rb1#

#108. **1...Qg1+ 2. Nxg1 Nf2#**

#109. **1...Kh7** *and* **2...g6#**

#110. **1...Qg1+**
    (A) 2. Kf3 Bb7#
    (B) 2. Kd2 Ne4#

#111. **1...Bxb3+**
    (A) 2. Kxb3 Qa4#
    (B) 2. Kb1 Qa2#
    (C) 2. Kd2 Qh6#

#112. **1...Bc3+**
    (A) 2. Kxc3 d1/N#
    (B) 2. Kb1 d1/Q#

#113. **1...Ng3+ 2. hxg3 Rh5#**

#114. **1...Rb2** *and* **2...Rc6#**

#115. **1...Bf4+ (A) 2. Qxf4 Qa5#**
    (B) 2. Re3 Rd1#

#116. **1...Qa6+ (A) 2. g6 Qxg6#**
    (B) 2. e6 Qxe6#
    (C) 2. Ke4 Qd3#

#117. **1...Qf1+ (A) 2. Kxf1 Rh1#**
    (B) 2. Rxf1 Ne2#

#118. **1...Nb3+ (A) 2. Bxb3 Qa1#**
    (B) 2. Kb1 Ned2#

#119. **1...b3 (A) 2. cxb3 Kxb3#**
    (B) 2. Ba2 Kxc2#

#120. **1...Qa4+ 2. Kd3 Nc1#**

#121. **1...b5+** *and* **2...Qa6#**

#122. **1...Rxe2** *and* **2...Be8#**

#123. **1...Rf5+ (A) 2. Kxe4 Re5#**
    (B) 2. Kc4 Nd2#

#124. **1...Qa7** *and* **2...Rxf1#**

#125. **1...gxh1/B 2. Kxg1 Ke2#**

#126. **1...Bb2 (A) 2. Bxb4 Qa1#**
      (B) 2. Bxb2 Qa2#

#127. **1...Qg1+ 2. Kxg1 Re1#**

#128. **1...Rxa3+ (A) 2. Kxa3 Qa1#**
      (B) 2. Qxa3 Qa5# ·
      (C) 2. Kb5 a6#

#129. **1...Kh1** *zugswang.*
      (A) 2. Ne2-*moves* **Ng3#**
      (B) 2. Nc4-*moves* **Ne3#**

#130. 1...Qc4+
      There are eight ways to take the Queen:
      (A) 2. Kxc4 Re4#
      (B) 2. Qxc4 Ne2#
      (C) 2. R6xc4 Ne6#
      (D) 2. R3xc4 Rxd3#
      (E) 2. Bxc4 Nxc6#
      (F) 2. Naxc4 Nxb5#
      (G) 2. Nbxc4 Rd5#
      (H) 2. dxc4 Re4#

#131. **1...Nf3** (*threatens* **2...Nh2#**)
      2. gxf3 Qh3#

#132. *White has just played* **1. b2-b4**
      allowing the en passant capture:
      1...cxb3+ 2. Ka1 Bb2#

#133. **1...Rxh3+ (A) 2. Kxh3 Qh5#**
      (B) 2. gxh3 Qf2# *An epaulet mate.*

#134. **1...Nb3** *and* **2...Qa1#**

#135. **1...Ng2** (*threatens* **2...Ne3#**)
      2. Kxg2 f1/Q#

#136. **1...Nd4+ (A) 2. Kf1 Qg2#**
      (B) 2. Bxd4 (*or* **2. Kd2**)
      2...Qd3#

#137. **1...Qxc5+ 2. Kxc5 Ne6#**

#138. **1...Rxe4** (*threatens* **2...Re1#** *and*
      2...Ref4#)
      (A) 2. Rxe4 Bxe4#
      (B) 2. Rh8+ Re8#

#139. **1. Be3 zugswang.**
      (A) 2. Nb2 Bc5#
      (B) 2. Nb4 Bc1#

#140. **1...Nd5** (*threatening* **2...Rd1#**)
      The Knight has to be taken and there are eight ways to do it:
      (A) 2. Kxd5 Rd1#
      (B) 2. Qxd5 Qa1#
      (C) 2. Rxd5 Qxc4#
      (D) 2. Bxd5 e5#
      (E) 2. Ncxd5 Nxe6#
      (F) 2. Nfxd5 Rxe4#
      (G) 2. exd5 Be5#
      (H) 2. cxd5 Qd3#

#141. **1.Qc4** (*threatens* **2...Qe2#**)
      (A) 2. Bd3 Qxc1#
      (B) 2. Bd1 Qh4#

#142. **1...Rxf1+ 2. Kxf1 Qh1#**

#143. **1...Rb4** *and* **2...Raxa4#**

#144. **1...Rf5+**
      (A) 2. Kxf5 Qf6#
      (B) 2. Ke3 Qe1#
      A swallow's tail and an epaulet.

#145. **1...Qh3+**
      (A) 2. Kxh3 Bf1#
      (B) 2. Kg1 Qf1#

#146. **1...Re2+ 2. Kxe2 Qd2#**
The Swallow's Tail mate, a close relative of the epaulet.

#147. **1...Qg2+ (A) 2. Qxg2 Ne2#**
(B) 2. Rxg2 Nh3#

#148. **1...Qe5** (*threatening* **2...Rd1#.**)
(A) 2. Qxh4+ Rxh4#
(B) 2. Qh2 Rf4#
(C) 2. Qe1 Rd2#
(D) 2. Kb2 Rc4#
(E) 2. exd4 Qxd4#

#149. **1...Rd1+ (A) 2. Nxd1 Qc4#**
(B) 2. Qe1 Rxe1#
(C) 2. Ke2 Nd4#

#150. **1...b5** (*threatens* **2...Rf1#**)
(A) 2. Qxb5 Qxb5#
(B) 2. c3 Qe4#

#151. **1.Nf4+ Kg8 2. Rag2+ Kf8**
3. Rh8#

#152. **1. Qg7+ Rxg7 2. Re8+ Rg8**
3. Rxg8#

#153. **1. Nh6+ gxh6 2. Rg3+ Kf7**
(*or* **2...Kh8 3. Rxf8#**) **3. Re7#**

#154. **1. Qxf6+ Rxf6**
(*or* **1...Kg8 2. Qg7#**) **2. Rxd8+ Rf8 3. Rxf8#**

#155. **1. Qxf7+ Rxf7 2. Rd8+ Rf8**
3.Rxf8#

#156. **1. Qd8 Rxd8 2. f8/Q+ Rxf8**
3. Rxf8#

#157. **1. Nh6+ gxh6 2. Rg4+ Kh8**
3. Rxf8#

#158. **1. Qxb8 Rxb8 2. e8/Q+ Rxe8**
3. Rxe8#

#159. **1. Qxd8+ Rxd8 2. Re8+ Rxe8**
3.Rxe8#

#160. **1. g6+ hxg6 2. fxg6+ Ke8**
3. Re8#

#161. **1. Nh5+ gxh5 2. Qg5+ Kf8**
3. Rd8#

#162. **1. Qh7+ Ka1 2. Qh8 Kb1**
3. Qh1#

#163. **1. Nd7+ Ka8 2. Rc5** (*threatens*
3. Ra5#) **2...Re5 3. Rc8#**

#164. **1. Qxh7+ Kxh7 2. Rh4+ Bxh4**
3.Rxh4#

#165. **1. Ng6+ hxg6 2. Qg1** *and*
3. Qh2#

#166. **1. Rxh6+ Kxh6 2. Qf4+** *and*
3. Qh2#

#167. **1. Bg8** (*threatens* **2. Rh7#**)
1...Rxg8 2. Rxg8+ Kh7 3. R1g7#

#168. **1. Rg7+ Kh8 2. Rh7+ Kg8**
3. Rag7#

#169. **1. Qxh7+ Kxh7 2. Rh3+ Kg6**
3. Rg2#

#170. **1. Qh8+ Ke7 2. Ng6+ fxg6**
3. Qxg7#

#171. **1. Qg4+ Bg5 2. Qxg5+ fxg5**
3. Rh8#

#172. **1. Qh8+ Kxh8 2. Rxh5+ Kg8
3. Rh8#**

#173. **1. Qxb6+ cxb6 2. Rxb6+ Kc7
3. Rb7#**
The swallow's tail mate.

#174. **1. Qxf8+ Kxf8 2. Bh6+ Kg8
3. Re8#**

#175. **1. Qg7+ Bxg7 2. Rxd8+ Bf8
3. Rxf8#**

#176. **1. Rf4+ Kh8 2. Ng6+ hxg6
3.Rh4#**
Greco's h-file corridor mate with Bishop and heavy piece. It goes back to 1619.

#177. **1. Bf5** *followed by* **2. h4+** *and* **3. Rh7#**

#178. **1. Bh6+ Kg8 2. Bxf7+ Kxf7
3. Qa2#**

#179. **1. Qc5+ Kd8 2. e7+ Kd7
3. Bf5#**

#180. **1. Qg7+ Ke8 2. Nd6+ cxd6
3. Bg6#**

#181. **1. Rxh6+ gxh6 2. Bb2+ Rf6
3. Bxf6#**

#182. **1. Bd8** *followed by*
**2. b6+ cxb6
3. Bxb6#** *Black can't stop it.*

#183. **1. Nf8+ Kh8 2. Qh7+ Nxh7
3. Ng6#**

#184. *The quiet move,* **1. Kf1,** *sets things up:*
1...Kxh2 2. Bd6+ Kh1 3.Nf2#
If Black plays a different first move, White reverses with **2. Nf2+** *and* **3. Bd6#**

#185. **1. Re8+ Kxe8 2. Rg8+ Ke7
3. Nf5#**

#186. **1. Ne8** (*threatens* **2. Rg7#**) **1...hxg4
2. Rg7+ (A) 2. ...Kf5 3. Nd6#
(B) 2. ...Kh5 3. Nxf6#**

#187. **1. Qxf7+ Rxf7 2. Rxf7+ Kh8
3. Ng6#**

#188. **1. Qxh6+ gxh6 (1...Kxh6 2. Rh1#)
2. Nf6+ Kh8 3. Rxg8#**
The Arabian Rook and Knight mate.

#189. **1. Nc5+ Kb8 (1...Kd8 2. Qd7#)
2. Qc8+ (A) 2...Ka7 2. Qxb7#
(B) 2...Kxc8 3.Rf8#**

#190. **1. Ne7+ Kh8 2. Qxh7+ Kxh7
3. Rh4#** *Anastasia's mate.*

#191. **1. Qxg7+ Nxg7 2. Rh6+ Kg8
3. Ne7#**

#192. **1. Ne7+ Kh8 2. Qxh7+ Kxh7
3. Rh4#**

#193. **1. Qxf7+ Rxf7 2. Ng6+ Kg8
3. Rh8#**

#194. **1. Rh8+ Kxh8 2. Qh5+ Kg8
3. Qh7#**

#195. **1. Ra8+ Kxa8 2. Qa1+ Kb8
3. Qa7#**

#196. **1. Rh7+ Kxh7 2. Qf7+ Kh8
3. Qg7#**

#197. **1. Rxg5** (*threatens* **2. Qxg7#**)
1. ...hxg5 2. f6 *and* **3. Qxg7#**

#198. **1. Rg8+ Kxg8 2. Qg5+ Kf8
3. Qg7#**

#199. **1. b6+ Ka6 2. Qa8+ Kb5
3. Qa5#**

#200. **1. h4+ Kxh4 2. Rxh5+ gxh5
3. Qxh5#**

#201. **1. Qf4+ Kd5 2. c4+ Kc6
3. Qc7#**

#202. **1. Qh8+ Qg8 2. Rxf7+ Kxf7
3. Qf6#** *The swallow's tail mate.*

#203. **1. Re8** (*threatens* **2. Qg7#**)
**1...Qxe8 2. Qf6+ Rg7
3. Qxg7#**

#204. **1. Bc6+ Qxc6 (1...Kd8 2. Qd7#)
2. Rxf8+ Kxf8 3. Qxe7#**

#205. **1. Rxc8+ Bxc8 2. Bf4** *and*
3. Qb8#

#206. **1. Qh6+ Ke8 (1...Kg8 2. Qg7#)
2. Qh8+ Kd7 3. Qb8#**

#207. **1. Nc7+ Qxc7 2. Qe6+ Be7
3. Qxe7#**

#208. **1. Rh4 Rg7 2. Bf8** *and the*
Queen mates on g7 or h7.

#209. **1. Qf4+ Kg8 2. Qf7+ Kh8
3. Qg7#**

#210. **1. Qxd6+ Kg8 2. Re8+ Qf8
3. Qxf8#**

#211. **1. Bf8** (*threatens* **2. Qxa7#**)
**1...Rb7
2. Rd8+ Rb8 3. Qxa7#**

#212. **1. Bxh5** (*threatens* **2. Qg6#**)
1...Kxh5 2. Qh7+ Kg4 3. Qh3#

#213. **1. Bxh7+ Nxh7 (1...Kh8 2.Nf7#)
2. Qf7+ Kh8 3. Ng6#**

#214. **1. Bxd4+ Nxd4 2. Qf6+ Kg8
3. Nh6#**

#215. **1. Nb3 h2 2. Kb6 h1/Q
3. Nc5#**

#216. **1. Ne2 Ka1 2. Nc1 a2
3. Nb3#**

#217. **1. Rh3 gxh3 (1...g3 2. Ng4#)
2. Ng4 h2 3 Nf2#**

#218. **1. Qxh7+ Nxh7 2. Nxf7+ Nxf7
3. Ng6#**
White's 1st and 2nd moves can be re-
versed.

#219. **1. Nd6+ Kd8 (1...Kf8 2. Qh6#)
2. Qe8+ Rxe8 3. Nf7#**

#220. **1.Qxb8+Bxb8 (1...Kxb8 2.Rc8#)
2. Nb6+ Ka7 3. Ndc8#**

#221. **1. Rxa6+ bxa6 2. b7+ Ka7
3. b8/Q#**

#222. **1. Qa4+ Kxa4 2. Rxa7+ Kb5 3 a4#**

#223. **1. Qg7+ Rxg7 2. Nh6+ Kh8 3. fxg7#**

#224. **1. Bh6+ Kxh6 2. Qf8+ Kh5 3. g4#**

#225. **1. Ra6+ Kxa6 2. Nc5+ Ka5 3. b4#**

#226. **1. Rh3+ Nh5 2. Rxh5+ gxh5 3. g5#**

#227. **1. Nh5+ Kg8 2. f6 hxg5 3. f7#**

#228. **1. Qf8+ Rxf8 2. Rxf8+ Kd7 3. e6#**

#229. **1. Rh8+ Kxh8 2. Rh6+ Kg8 3. Qxg7#**

#230. **1. Rh8+ Kxh8 2. Qh6+ Bh7 3. Qxg7#**

#231. **1. Ra8+ Kxa8 2. Qa6+ Kb8 3. Qxb7#**

#232. **1. Qg8+ Kh6 2. Qdf8+ Qg7 3. Qh8#**

#233. **1. Qxh6+ Kg8 (1...Kxh6 2.Bxf6#) 2. Bxf6 Rh7** (*else Queen mates at g7 or h8*) **3. Qxh7#** *A pin mate.*

#234. **1. Qxf7+ Kxf7 2. R1h7+ Ke8 3. Bg6#**

#235. **1. Qh8+ Kxh8 2. Nxf7+ Kg8 3. Nh6#**

#236. **1. Qe8+ Kxe8 2. Nf6+ Kd8 3. Re8#**

#237. **1. Qh6+ Bxh6 2. Ng5+ Kh8 3. Rh7#**

#238. **1. Qe8+ Kxe8 2. Bc6+ Kf8 3. Re8#**

#239. **1. Qe8+ Kxe8 2. Bb5+ Kd8 3. Re8#**

#240. **1. Qd8+ Kxd8 2. Bg5+ Ke8 3. Rd8#**

#241. **1. Qg8+ Kxg8 2. Be6+ Kh8 3. Rg8#**

#242. **1. Rxg7+ Kxg7 2. Rg8+ Kxg8 3. Rg1#**

#243. **1. Rf8+ Rxf8 2. Rxg6+ Rf6 3. Bxf6#**

#244. **1. Kc2 Nd2 2. Nd4 N-moves 3. Nb3#**

#245. **1. Kf6 cxd6 2. Ke7 dxc5 3. Nf6#**

#246. **1. Kd3 (A) 1...Kc5 2. Qa5#**
(B) 1...Ke5 2. Qg5#
(C) 1...c5 2. Qg5+ e5 3. Qg8#
(D) 1...e5 2. Qa5+ c5 3. Qa8#

#247. **1. Bf2 Kb4 2. Bd4 Ka3 3.Bc5#**
A little King and Bishop duel. Bishop wins.

#248. **1. Bh1 f4 2. Bxe4 f3 3.Bxb7#**
A Bishop and Pawn duel. No contest. Bishop wins again.

#249. **1. Rc5**
(A) 1...dxc5 2. c4 dxc3
3. Nxc3#
(B) 1...d5 2. c3 dxc3 3. Nxc3#

#250. **1. Qg8 Rxg8 2. Bxg8 Kxc2**
3. Bxh7#

#251. **1...Rf1** (*threatens* 2...Qxc1#)
2. Rxf1 Qe1+ 3. Rxe1 Rxe1#

#252. **1...Bf6** (*threatens* 2...Qxg5#)
2. Nf3 (*or* 2. exf6 *or* 2. gxf6)
2...Kg6 *and* **3...Qh7#**
Black's first move seals the 6th
rank so White cannot play Qxe6
with check.

#253. **1...Qxe3+ 2. Bxe3 fxe3** *and*
3...Bf2#

#254. **1...Qxb2+ 2. Rxb2 Bc2+**
3. Ra2 Bxc3#

#255. **1...Qd1+ 2. Rxd1 Nc2+**
3. Nxc2 Rxd1#

#256. **1...Bf3+ 2.Bxf3** (*or* 2.Kg1 Qg2#)
2...Be5 *and* **3...Qxh2#**

#257. **1...Qa1+ 2. Kxa1** (2.Kc2 Qxc1#)
2...dxc1/Q+ 3. Bb1 Qc3#

#258. **1...f6 2. Ra1 Rg5** (*threatens*
3...Rxh5#) **3. fxg5+ fxg5#**

#259. **1...Qxg2+ 2. Kxg2 Nf4+**
3. Kg1 Nh3#

#260. **1...Rc6+** (A) **2. Kd7 Rb6+**
3. Kd8 Rd6#
(B) **2. Ke5 Bc2** *and* **3...f6#**

#261. **1...Bxd4+**
(A) 2. Qe3 Bxe3+ 3. Rf2
(*or* 3. Kh1 Qxf1#) 3...Ra1#
(B) 2. cxd4 Qxf1+ 3. Kxf1 c1#

#262. **1...Nh4+ 2. Rxh4 Rxg3+**
3. Kxg3 Re3#

#263. **1...Qa4+** (A) **2. Kc1 Bxd3**
3. Qd1 Qxa3# (B) **2. Ke2**
Bxd3+ 3. Kxd3 (*or* 3. Kf3
Qg4#) **3...Qc4#**

#264. **1...Rc2** (*threatens* 2...Na3#)
(A) 2. Rxc2 Rd1+ 3. Rc1 Na3#
(B) 2. Kxc2 Rd2+ 3. Kb3 Rb2#

#265. **1...Qxf2+ 2. Bxf2 Rxc1+**
3. Be1 Rxe1#

#266. **1...Be4** (*threatens* 2...Qg2#)
(A) 2. Qf3 Bxf3 *and* 3...Qg2#
(B) 2. Qf1 Ne2+ 3. Qxe2 Qg2#
From a scholastics tournament. The
kid playing Black sat for over twenty
minutes and worked it out.

#267. **1...Bxf3+ 2. Kxf3**
(2. Kg1 e1/Q#)
2...e1/N+ 3. Kg4 h5#

#268. **1...Rh1+ 2. Kxh1 Qh3+**
3. Kg1 Qxg2#

#269. **1...Qg5** (*threatens* 2...Qg2#)
(A) 2. Nxg5 Nxf2+ 3. Kg1
Nh3#
(B) 2. Rg1 Qxg1+ 3. Nxg1
Ng3#

#270. **1...d4+**
(A) 2. Kxd4 Qe4+ 3. Kc5 b6#
(B) 2. cxd4 Qe4+ 3. Kd2 Qxd4#
(C) 2. Kf4 Qe4+ *and* 3...Qg4#

#271. **1...Nc1+ 2. Kb1** (**2. Ka3 Qb3#**)
2...Qa2+ 3. Kxc1 Qa1#

#272. **1...Qa1+ 2. Ra2 Rxa4+**
3. bxa4 (or **3. Kxa4 Qxa2#**)
3...Qc3# *An epaulet mate.*

#273. **1...Ba2+ 2. Kxa2 Qg8+**
3. Kb1 Qb3#

#274. **1...Re2+ 2. Nxe2 Ne4+**
3. Kd1 Nf2#

#275. **1...Qxe4** (*threatens* **2...Nxg2+**
and **3...Qe1#**)
2. dxe4 d3 *and*
3...Re2# *is unstoppable.*

#276. **1...Ra1+ 2. Bxa1 Qa7** *and*
3...Qa2#

#277. **1...Bd8+ 2. Bxd8** (**2. g5 Bxg5#**
2...e1/N *with* **3...Ng2#** *or else*
3...Nf3#

#278. **1...Be4** (*threatens both* **2...Qxd4#**
and **2...Rb1#**)
2. Rxe4 Qh1+
3. Qd1 Qxd1#

#279. **1...Ng5** (*releases stalemate and
creates zugzswang*)
2. hxg5 Bxb6
3. g6 Be3#

#280. **1...Qc4+ 2. Kd6** (**2. Kb6 Qb4#**)
2...Qc7+ 3. Kxd5 Qc6#

#281. **1...Qb5+ 2. Ka3 Rc4** (*threatens*
3...Ra4#) **3. Qd1 Qb4#**

#282. **1...Kc7** *followed by* **2...Ra8** *and*
3...Ra1# *Not* **1...Rxf7?**
*when White can drag things out
by* **2. Ne7!**

#283. **1...Nd2+ (A) 2. Kb2 Qb1+**
3. Kc3 Ne4# (B) 2. Kc1 Qb1+
3. Kxd2 Bb4#
*A switch back combined with a
criss-cross mate.*

#284. **1...Qa4** (*threatens* **2...Qxa2#**)
**(A) 2. a3 Qxb3+ 3. Ka1
Rxa3# (B) 2. bxa4 Rb6+ 3.
Ka1 Nc2# (C) 2. Kb2** (*or* **2.
Re3**) **2...Qxa2+** *and* **3...Qc2#**

#285. **1...Rd2+ 2. Nxd2 Qa2+** *and*
3...Qxd2#

#286. **1...Qxb2+ 2. Nxb2 Nc3+**
3. Ka1 Nxc2#

#287. **1...Qxb2+ (A) 2. Rxb2 Rc1+**
3. Rb1 b2# (B) 2. Kxb2 Rc2+
and **3...Rxa2#**

#288. **1.Rg1+ 2. Kxg1 Rg8+**
3. Kf2 Rg2#

#289. **1...Bb3** (*threatens* **2...Qxa2#**)
2. cxb3 (**2. axb3 Qa1#**)
2...Rc1+ 3. Rxc1 Rxc1#

#290. **1...Qh3+ 2. Kxh3 Bf1+**
3. Kh4 f5#

#291. **1...Rxa3+ 2. Kxa3 Qc5+**
3. Ka2 Qa7#
*Greco's mating pattern on the
Rook's file.*

#292. **1...Qa5+ 2. Ba4 Qxa4+**
3. bxa4 Ra3#

#293. **1...Rxc2+ 2. Bxc2 Qb4+**
3. Ke3 Qd4#

#294. **1...Nb3+ 2. axb3 Qa3+
3. bxa3 Ra2#**

#295. **1...Rxb3+ 2. cxb3
(2. Ka2 Rb2#)
2...Qd3+ 3. Ka2 Qxb3#**

#296. **1...Bb7** (*threatens* **2...h1/Q#**)
(A) 2. Kh7 Rg4 *and* **3...h1/Q#**
**(B) 2. Rxb7 h1/Q+ 3. Rh7
Qa8#**

#297. **1...Re3+ 2. Kxd4 Nc2+
3. Kc4 b5#**

#298. **1...Nxc2+ 2. Kb1 Nd4+
3. Kc1** (*or* **3. Ka1 Nb3#**)
3...Ne2#

#299. **1...Ba8 2. b7 Kxb7
3. Kd5 Qe5#**

#300. **1...Rf1+ 2. Kxf1 Qh1+
3. Kf2 Ng4#**

#301. **1. Be4+ Kg5 2. Rg7+ Kh6
3. Rh7+ Kg5 4. h4#**

#302. **1. Rxa7+ Kxa7 2. Rb7+ Ka8
3. Ra7+ Kxa7 4. Qb7#**

#303. **1. Qh6+ Kxh6 2. Ng4+ Kg7
3. Nh5+ Kh8 4. g7#**

KASPAROV EXPRESS™

SAITEK - The World Leader in Intelligent Electronic Games

VERSATILE AND FUN - An amazing 384 level/setting combinations includes fun levels for novices and challenging levels for experienced players. Economic powerful, and pocket size (approximately 5" x 61/2" x 1') this game is an unbeatable easy traveling companion.
GREAT INEXPENSIVE TRAVEL COMPANION! - Features different playing styles and strengths, 5 special coach modes, and teaching levels! Sensory-style chess board, peg type pieces, folding lid, LCD screen, take back and hint features, built-in chess clock that keeps track of time for both sides, and self-rating system. Memory holds an unfinished game for up to two years, gives you the complete package in an economical, handy travel-ready unit.

To order, send just $49.95 for the Express.

KASPAROV TRAVEL CHAMPION 2100

SAITEK - The World Leader in Intelligent Electronic Games

THE WORLD'S MOST POWERFUL HAND-HELD CHESS COMPUTER ANYWHERE! - This **super program** and **integrated training system** has an **official USCF rating of 2334!** This **awesome program** can beat over 99% of all chess players, yet it's still great for the novice. LCD shows principal variation, evaluation, search depth, and search mode counts.
64 SKILL LEVELS - 64 levels of skill and handicapping give you tons of **options** and **versatility**: Play against beginning, intermediate or advanced opponents (includes tournament time controls), play Blitz or Tournament, choose Active, Passive, or Complete style, or Tournament Opening Book, select **Brute Force** algorithm or the advanced Selective Search. Match your skill to the correct level for most **challenging** chess. You want it - it's all here!

To order, send just $129.95 for the Kasparov Travel Champion 2100.

KASPAROV CHESS GK2100™
SAITEK - The World Leader in Intelligent Electronic Games

THE BEST VALUE MONEY CAN BUY! - The **fabulous** Kasparov GK2100 is the **most popular** chess computer we sell. Using a super high speed **RISC** computer chip and rated at a **2334** USCF rating, you'll have consistent challenges and excitement. Coaching features and fun levels makes it suitable for novices; masters and experts will want to choose higher levels.

GREAT DESIGN - Packaged in a sleek, handsome cabinet suitable for your living room. No need to find a partner to play - **take on the Champion**!

POWERFUL PROGRAM FEATURES - **64 levels of play** include sudden death, tournament, problem solving and beginner's. Shows intended move and position evaluation, take back up to 50 moves, and user selectable **book openings library**. Also choose from **Active, Passive, Tournament, complete book, no book.** Select the high speed **Selective Search** or play against the powerful **Brute Force.** program. Thinks in opponents time for best realism. Shutoff, shut on memory - remembers game for 1 year!

GREAT FOR BEGINNERS AND MASTERS ALIKE! - This **awesome program** can beat over 99% of all regular chess players, yet it is still suitable for beginners and intermediate players: Simply set the skill level to the appropriate strength for the best challenges. Matching your skill to the correct level of play ensures a **challenging** and **exciting** game.

EVEN MORE FEATURES - Opening library of 35,000 moves, **large LCD** shows full information and keeps track of playing time. Modern ergonomic design goes well in living room.

To order, send $199.95 for the Kasparov Chess GK2100

CARDOZA PUBLISHING CHESS BOOKS

- OPENINGS -

WINNING CHESS OPENINGS by Bill Robertie - Shows concepts and best opening moves of more than 25 essential openings from Black's and White's perspectives: King's Gambit, Center Game, Scotch Game, Giucco Piano, Vienna Game, Bishop's Opening, Ruy Lopez, French, Caro-Kann, Sicilian, Alekhine, Pirc, Modern, Queen's Gambit, Nimzo-Indian, Queen's Indian, Dutch, King's Indian, Benoni, English, Bird's, Reti's, and King's Indian Attack. Examples from 25 grandmasters and champions including Fischer and Kasparov. 144 pages, $9.95

WORLD CHAMPION OPENINGS by Eric Schiller - This serious reference work covers the essential opening theory and moves of every major chess opening and variation as played by *all* the world champions. Reading as much like an encyclopedia of the must-know openings crucial to every chess player's knowledge as a powerful tool showing the insights, concepts and secrets as used by the greatest players of all time, *World Champion Openings (WCO)* covers an astounding 100 crucial openings in full conceptual detail (with 100 actual games from the champions themselves)! *A must-have book for serious chess players.* 384 pages, $18.95

STANDARD CHESS OPENINGS by Eric Schiller - The new definitive standard on opening chess play in the 20th century, this comprehensive guide covers every important chess opening and variation ever played and currently in vogue. In all, more than 3,000 opening strategies are presented! Differing from previous opening books which rely almost exclusively on bare notation, *SCO* features substantial discussion and analysis on each opening so that you learn and understand the concepts behind them. Includes more than 250 completely annotated games (including a game representative of each major opening) and more than 1,000 diagrams! For modern players at any level, this is the standard reference book necessary for competitive play. *A must have for serious chess players!!!* 768 pages, $24.95

UNORTHODOX CHESS OPENINGS by Eric Schiller - The exciting guide to all the major unorthodox openings used by chess players, contains more than 1,500 weird, contentious, controversial, unconventional, arrogant, and outright strange opening strategies. From their tricky tactical surprises to their bizarre names, these openings fly in the face of tradition. You'll meet such openings as the Orangutang, Raptor Variation, Halloween Gambit, Double Duck, Frankenstein-Dracula Variation, and even the Drunken King! These openings are a sexy and exotic way to spice up a game and a great weapon to spring on unsuspecting and often unprepared opponents. More than 750 diagrams show essential positions. 528 pages, $24.95

GAMBIT OPENING REPERTOIRE FOR WHITE by Eric Schiller - Chessplayers who enjoy attacking from the very first move are rewarded here with a powerful repertoire of brilliant gambits. Starting off with 1.e4 or 1.d4 and then using such sharp weapons such as the Göring Gambit (Accepted and Declined), Halasz Gambit, Alapin Gambit, Ulysses Gambit, Short Attack and many more, to put great pressure on opponents, Schiller presents a complete attacking repertoire to use against the most popular defenses, including the Sicilian, French, Scandinavian, Caro-Kann, Pirc, Alekhine, and other Open Game positions. 192 pages, $14.95.

GAMBIT OPENING REPERTOIRE FOR BLACK by Eric Schiller - For players that like exciting no-holds-barred chess, this versatile gambit repertoire shows Black how to take charge with aggressive attacking defenses against any orthodox first White opening move; 1.e4, 1.d4 and 1.c4. Learn the Scandinavian Gambit against 1.e4, the Schara Gambit and Queen's Gambit Declined variations against 1.d4, and some flank and unorthodox gambits also. Black learns the secrets of seizing the initiative from White's hands, usually by investing a pawn or two, to begin powerful attacks that can send White to early defeat. 176 pages, $14.95.

COMPLETE DEFENSE TO QUEEN PAWN OPENINGS by Eric Schiller - This aggressive counterattacking repertoire covers Black opening systems against virtually every chess opening except for 1.e4 (including most flank games), based on the exciting and powerful Tarrasch Defense, an opening that helped bring Championship titles to Kasparov and Spassky. Black learns to effectively use the Classical Tarrasch, Symmetrical Tarrasch, Asymmetrical Tarrasch, Marshall and Tarrasch Gambits, and Tarrasch without Nc3, to achieve an early equality or even an outright advantage in the first few moves. 288 pages, $16.95.

COMPLETE DEFENSE TO KING PAWN OPENINGS *by Eric Schiller* - Learn a complete defensive system against 1.e4. This powerful repertoire not only limits White's ability to obtain any significant opening advantage but allows Black to adopt the flexible Caro-Kann formation, the favorite weapon of many of the greatest chess players. All White's options are explained in detail, and a plan is given for Black to combat them all. Analysis is up-to-date and backed by examples drawn from games of top stars. Detailed index lets you follow the opening from the point of a specific player, or through its history. 240 pages, $16.95.

SECRETS OF THE SICILIAN DRAGON by *GM Eduard Gufeld and Eric Schiller* - The mighty Dragon Variation of the Sicilian Defense is one of the most exciting openings in chess. Everything from opening piece formation to the endgame, including clear explanations of all the key strategic and tactical ideas, is covered in full conceptual detail. Instead of memorizing a jungle of variations, you learn the really important ideas behind the opening, and how to adapt them at the chessboard. Special sections on the heroes of the Dragon show how the greatest players handle the opening. The most instructive book on the Dragon written! 208 pages, $14.95.

SECRETS OF THE KING'S INDIAN *by Eduard Gufeld and Eric Schiller* - The King's Indian is the single most popular opening and offers great opportunities for spectacular attacks and clever defenses. You'll learn the fundamental concepts, critical ideas, and hidden resources along with the opening traps and typical tactical and strategic mistakes. All major variations are covered, including the Classical, Petrosian, Saemisch, Averbakh, Four Pawns, Fianchetto and unconventional lines. You'll learn how the strategies and tactics were applied in the brilliant games of the most famous players, and how to apply them to your own game. 240 pgs, $14.95.

HYPERMODERN OPENING REPERTOIRE FOR WHITE *by Eric Schiller* - Instead of placing pawns in the center of the board as traditional openings advise, this complete opening repertoire for White shows you how to stun opponents by "allowing" Black to occupy the center with its pawns, while building a crushing phalanx from the flanks, ready to smash the center apart with Black's slightest mistake. White's approach is simple to learn because White almost always develops pieces in the same manner, but can be used against all defenses no matter what Black plays! Diagrams and explanations illustrate every concept, with games from the greatest players showing the principles in action. The Réti and English openings form the basis of the Hypermodern and lead to games with brilliant sacrifices and subtle maneuvering. 304 pages, $16.95.

- MIDDLEGAME/TACTICS/WINNING CONCEPTS -

10 MOST COMMON CHESS MISTAKES, and How to Fix Them *by Larry Evans* - This fascinating collection of 218 errors, oversights, and outright blunders, will not only show you the price that great players pay for violating basic principles, but how you can avoid these mistakes in your own game. You'll be challenged to choose between two moves; the right one, or the one actually played in the game. From neglecting development, king safety, misjudging threats, and premature attacks, to impulsiveness, snatching pawns, and basic inattention, you will get a complete course in exactly where you go wrong and how to fix it. 256 pages, $14.95.

303 TRICKY CHESS TACTICS *by Fred Wilson and Bruce Alberston* - Both a fascinating challenge and great training tool, this is a fun and entertaining collection of two and three move tactical surprises for the advanced beginner, intermediate, and expert player. Tactics are arranged by difficulty so that a player may measure progress as he advances from simple to the complex positions. The examples, drawn from actual games, illustrate a wide range of chess tactics from old classics right up to the 1990's. 192 pages, $12.95.

ENCYCLOPEDIA OF CHESS WISDOM, The Essential Concepts and Strategies of Smart Chess Play *by Eric Schiller* - The most important concepts, strategies, tactics, wisdom, and thinking that every chessplayer must know, plus the gold nuggets of knowledge behind every attack and defense, is collected together in one highly focused volume. From opening, middle and endgame strategy, to psychological warfare and tournament tactics, the *Encyclopedia of Chess Wisdom* forms the blueprint of power play and advantage at the chess board. Step-by-step, the reader is taken through the thinking behind each essential concept, and through examples, discussions, and diagrams, shown the full impact on the game's direction. You even learn how to correctly study chess to become a chess master. 400 pages, $19.95.

AWESOME CHESS MOVES *By Eric Schiller* - This collection of brilliant ideas from real tournaments are not just regular combinations or tactical swindles, but moves of stunning originality. Schiller has selected 100 *awesome* moves, and through positions, examples, and clearly explained concepts, shows you how to improve your grasp of deep positional understandings and swashbuckling tactics. You'll learn how to reinforce your gut instincts to not just reach for the best move, but the *inspired* move. 224 pgs, $18.95.

WORLD CHAMPION TACTICS *by Leonid Shamkovich and Eric Schiller* - The authors show how the greatest players who ever lived used their entire arsenal of tactical weapons to bring opponents to their knees. Packed with fascinating strategems, 50 fully annotated games, and more than 200 diagrams, players learn not only the thinking and game plan behind the moves of the champions, but the insights that will allow them to use these brilliancies in their own games. Each tactical concept is fully explained with examples and game situations from the champions themselves. 304 pages, $18.95.

WORLD CHAMPION COMBINATIONS *by Keene and Schiller* - Learn the insights, concepts and moves of the greatest combinations ever by the greatest players who ever lived. From Morphy to Alekhine, to Fischer to Kasparov, the incredible combinations and brilliant sacrifices of the 13 World Champions are collected here in the most insightful combinations book written. Packed with fascinating strategems, 50 annotated games, and great practical advice for your own games, this is a great companion guide to *World Champion Openings.* 264 pages, $16.95.

WINNING CHESS TACTICS *by Bill Robertie* - 14 chapters of winning tactical concepts show the complete explanations and thinking behind every tactical concept: pins, single and double forks, double attacks, skewers, discovered and double checks, multiple threats - and other crushing tactics to gain an immediate edge over opponents. Learn the power tools of tactical play to become a stronger player. Includes guide to chess notation. 128 pages, $9.95

- BEGINNING AND GENERAL CHESS BOOKS -

BEGINNING CHESS PLAY *by Bill Robertie* - Step-by-step approach uses 113 diagrams to teach novices the basic principles of chess. Covers opening, middle and end game strategies, principles of development, pawn structure, checkmates, openings and defenses, how to write and read chess notation, join a chess club, play in tournaments, use a chess clock, and get rated. Two annotated games illlustrate strategic thinking for easy learning. 144 pages, $9.95

KEENE ON CHESS *by Raymond Keene* - Complete step-by-step course shows how to play and deepen one's understanding of chess while keeping the game fun and exciting. Fascinating chapters on chess heroes and lessons you can learn from these greats, basic chess openings, strategy, tactics, the best games of chess ever played, and the history of chess round out your education. You'll also learn how to use chess notation and all the basic concepts of game play – castling, pawn promotion, putting an opponent into check, the five ways of drawing or stalemating games, en passant, actual checkmate, and much more. 320 pages, $18.95.

WHIZ KIDS TEACH CHESS *Edited by Eric Schiller* - Ten of today's greatest young stars, ranging from 10-17 years old–some perhaps to be future world champions–present a fascinating look on learning chess. Each tells of their successes, failures, world travels, and love of the game, show off their best moves, and even admit to their most embarrassing blunders. At the heart of this inspirational book targeted toward beginning, under-17 players, is a basic chess primer with large diagrams, clear explanations, and winning ideas. Features Jordy Mont-Reynaud (14), who smashed Bobby Fischer's record by over two years to become the youngest USCF Master, Vinay Bhat (12), Gabe Kahane (16), the Karnazes' twins (10), Irina Krush (15), Asuka Nakamura (11), Hikaru Nakamura (10), and Jennifer Shahade (16). 128 large format pages, $14.95.

THE BASICS OF WINNING CHESS *by Jacob Cantrell* - A great first book of chess, in one easy reading, beginner's learn the moves of the pieces, the basic rules and principles of play, the standard openings, and both Algebraic and English chess notation. The basic ideas of the winning concepts and strategies of middle and end game play are shown as well. Includes example games of great champions. 64 pages, $4.95.

303 TRICKY CHECKMATES *by Fred Wilson and Bruce Alberston* - Both a fascinating challenge and great training tool, this collection of two, three and bonus four move checkmates is great for advanced beginning, intermediate and expert players. Mates are in order of difficulty, from the simple to very complex positions. Learn the standard patterns and stratagems for cornering the king: corridor and support mates, attraction and deflection sacrifices, pins and annihilation, the quiet move, and the dreaded *zugzwang*. Examples drawn from actual games, illustrate a wide range of chess tactics from old classics right up to the 1990's. 192 pgs, $12.95.

MASTER CHECKMATE STRATEGY *by Bill Robertie* - Learn the basic combinations, plus advanced, surprising and unconventional mates, the most effective pieces needed to win, and how to mate opponents with just a pawn advantage. also, how to work two rooks into an unstoppable attack; how to wield a queen advantage with deadly intent; how to coordinate pieces of differing strengths into indefensible positions of their opponents; when it's best to have a knight, and when a bishop to win. 144 pages, $9.95

BASIC ENDGAME STRATEGY: Kings, Pawns and Minor Pieces *by Bill Robertie* - Learn the mating principles and combinations needed to finish off opponents. From the four basic checkmates using the King with the queen, rook, two bishops, and bishop/knight combinations, to the King/pawn, King/Knight and King/Bishop endgames, you'll learn the essentials of translating small edges into decisive checkmates. Learn the 50-move rule, and the combinations of pieces that can't force a mate against a lone King. 144 pages, $12.95.

BASIC ENDGAME STRATEGY: Rooks and Queens by Bill Robertie - The companion guide to *Basic Endgame Strategy: Kings, Pawns and Minor Pieces*, you'll learn the basic mating principles and combinations of the Queen and Rook with King, how to turn middlegame advantages into victories, by creating passed pawns, using the King as a weapon, clearing the way for rook mates, and other endgame combinations. 144 pages, $12.95.

539 ESSENTIAL ENDGAME POSITIONS *by Eric Schiller* - From basic mates to sophisticated double-rook endgames, every important endgame concept is explained. Topics include every key combination of king and pawn endgames, bishops, knights, rooks, and queens, plus tricky endgames with no pawns. The thinking behind every position is explained in words (unlike diagram-only books) so that you'll learn which positions are winning, which are drawn, and which cannot be saved. Frequent diagrams show starting and target positions, so you can visualize end goals and steer the middlegame to a successful conclusion. 400 pages, $18.95.

USE ORDER FORM ON FOLLOWING PAGE

CARDOZA PUBLISHING ONLINE
www.cardozapub.com

To find out about our latest chess publications or to order books and software:
1. Go online: www.cardozapub.com
2. Use E-Mail: cardozapub@aol.com
3. Call toll free: 800-577-WINS (800-577-9467)

Our philosophy is to bring you the best quality chess books from the top authors and authorities in the chess world, featuring *words* (as opposed to hieroglyphics), *clear explanations* (as opposed to gibberish), *quality presentations* (as opposed to books simply slapped together), and *authoritative information*. And all this at reasonable prices. We hope you like the results.

CHESSCITY MAGAZINE - WWW.CHESSCITY.COM
Free Online Chess Magazine

Chess City Magazine is a sprawling metropolis of chess information, a magazine with the latest news and analysis, to gossip, trivia, and fun features. Travel around the world to visit the most fascinating chess competitions, preview books long they hit the shelves, and read columns on openings, middlegames, endings, tactics, strategies, mates, and more. Extensive excerpts from our books are available online. Visit often, because we'll be adding more features for your pleasure! Improve your chess knowledge with our articles and features on the opening, middlegame, endgame, strategy, tactics checkmates and more! Whether you're a beginner or master, you'll be able to improve your results with our tips.

Chess is a serious game, but it is also a lot of fun. *Chess City Magazine* presents trivia, photos, anecdotes, chess art, strange games, trivia and even a bit of gossip for your amusement and pleasure! Drop by often to visit!

Go to www.chesscity.com for details